THE GAME OF POLO.

MR JOHN WATSON.

Swan Electric Engraving

THE
GAME OF POLO

BY

T. F. DALE, M.A.

(*"Stoneclink" of the Field.*)

ILLUSTRATED BY

LILLIAN SMYTHE, CUTHBERT BRADLEY AND CRAWFORD WOOD.

POLO

HINTS TO A BEGINNER

WORDS of wrath at Polo spoken
    Should forgotten be next day;
They're a sure and certain token,
    Good the game and fast the play.
Least words said they're soonest mended,
    Never are they worth repeating;
Do not therefore be offended
    If defeated or defeating;
Keep your temper and your place,
    Gallop at your fastest pace.
If a man you chance to cross,
    You or he may take a "toss."
Learn the rules and play the game,
    Then you'll never be to blame;
If your pony stops to kick,
    Beat him with your Polo stick;
If he shuts up like a cur,
    Ride him with both whip and spur.
See your girths are new and strong,
    Stirrup leathers not too long,
Saddle-tree correctly fitting,
    Pay attention to your bitting.
If to win is your ambition,
    Keep yourself in good condition;
Choose a stick of proper length,
    Weight according to your strength;
Bearing this in mind you may
    P'r'aps in time improve your play.

Horses – Sports and Utility

The horse (*Equus ferus caballus*) is one of two extant subspecies of *Equus ferus*. It is an odd-toed ungulate mammal belonging to the taxonomic family 'Equidae'. The horse has evolved over the past 45 to 55 million years from a small multi-toed creature into the large, single-toed animal of today. Humans began to domesticate horses around 4000 BC, and their domestication is believed to have been widespread by 3000 BC. We, as humans have interacted with horses in a multitude of ways throughout history – from sport competitions and non-competitive recreational pursuits, to working activities such as police work, agriculture, entertainment and therapy. Horses have also been used in warfare, from which a wide variety of riding and driving techniques developed, using many different styles of equipment and methods of control. With this range of uses in mind, there is an equally extensive, specialized vocabulary used to describe equine-related concepts, covering everything from anatomy to life stages, size, colours, markings, breeds, locomotion, and behaviour.

Sporting events are some of the largest and best-known activities involving horses, and here – communication between human and horse is paramount. To aid this process, horses are usually ridden with a saddle on their backs to assist the rider with balance and positioning, and a bridle or related headgear to assist the rider in maintaining control. Historically, equestrians honed their craft through games and races;

providing skills needed for battle, as well as entertainment for home crowds. Today, these competitions have evolved into racing, dressage, eventing and show jumping – many of which have their origins in military training, focused on control and balance of both the horse and rider. Other sports, such as rodeo, developed from practical skills such as those needed on working ranches and stations. Horse racing of all types evolved from impromptu competitions between riders or drivers, and has since become a multi-million pound industry. It is watched in almost every nation of the world, in its three main forms: 'flat racing' (long, even stretches), 'steeplechasing' (racing over jumps) and 'harness racing' (where horses trot or pace whilst pulling a driver in a small, light cart). A major part of horse racing's economic importance lies in the gambling associated with it.

All forms of competition, requiring demanding and specialized skills from both horse and rider, resulted in the systematic development of specialized breeds and equipment for each sport. Horse shows, which have their origins in medieval European fairs, are held around the world. They host a huge range of classes, covering all of the mounted and harness disciplines, as well as 'In-hand' classes where the horses are led, rather than ridden, to be evaluated on their conformation. The method of judging varies with the discipline, but winning usually depends on style and ability of both horse and rider. Sports such as polo do not judge the horse itself, but rather use the horse as a partner for human competitors as a necessary part of the game. Although the horse requires specialized training to participate, the details of its performance are not judged, only the result of the rider's actions—be it getting a ball through a goal or some other task. A similar, historical example of sports partnerships between human and horse is 'jousting', in which the main goal is for one rider to unseat the other. This pastime is still practiced by some sportsmen today.

There are certain jobs that horses do very well, and no technology has yet developed to fully replace them. For example, mounted police horses are still effective for certain types of patrol duties and crowd control. Cattle ranches still require riders on horseback to round up cattle that are scattered across remote, rugged terrain. In more urban areas, horses used to be the main form of transport, in the form of pulling carriages, and are still extensively used (especially in the UK) for ceremonial functions, i.e. horse-drawn carriages transporting dignitaries, military personnel or even the royal family. Horses can also be used in areas where it is necessary to avoid vehicular disruption to delicate soil, such as nature reserves. They may also be the only form of transport allowed in wilderness areas, often because of the fact that horses are quieter than motorised vehicles, therefore impacting less on their surroundings. Although machinery has replaced horses in many parts of the world, an estimated 100 million horses, donkeys and mules are still used for agriculture and transportation in less developed areas. This number includes around 27 million working animals in Africa alone.

As well as these labour intensive uses, horses can also be incredibly valuable for therapy. People of all ages with physical and mental disabilities obtain beneficial results from association with horses. Therapeutic riding is used to mentally and physically stimulate disabled persons and help them improve their lives through improved balance and coordination, increased self-confidence, and a greater feeling of freedom and independence. Horses also provide psychological benefits to people whether they actually ride or not. 'Equine-assisted' or 'equine-facilitated' therapy is a form of experiential psychotherapy that uses horses as companion animals to assist people with mental illness, including anxiety disorders, psychotic disorders, mood disorders, behavioural difficulties, and those who are going through major life changes. There are also experimental programs using horses in prison settings. Exposure to horses appears to improve the behaviour of inmates and help reduce recidivism when they leave.

As a concluding note, one of the most important aspects of equine care is farriery; a specialist in equine hoof care. Horses aid humans in so many ways, it is important to ensure that they are properly equipped and cared for. Farriers have largely replaced blacksmiths (after this specialism mostly became redundant after the industrial revolution), and are highly skilled in both metalwork and horse anatomy. Historically, the jobs of farrier and blacksmith were practically synonymous, shown by the etymology of the word: farrier comes from Middle French *ferrier* (blacksmith), and from the Latin word *ferrum* (iron). Modern day farriers usually specialize in horseshoeing though, focusing their time and effort on the care of the horse's hoof, including trimming and balancing of the hoof, as well as the placing of the shoes. Additional tasks for the farrier include dealing with injured or diseased hooves and application of special shoes for racing, training or 'cosmetic' purposes. In countries such as the United Kingdom, it is illegal for people other than registered farriers to call themselves a farrier or to carry out any farriery work, the primary aim being 'to prevent and avoid suffering by and cruelty to horses arising from the shoeing of horses by unskilled persons.' This is not the case in all countries however, where horse protection is severely lacking.

We hope the reader enjoys this book.

TO JOHN WATSON, Esq., M.F.H.

DEAR WATSON,

It is only just that this book should be inscribed to you, since but for you it would never have been written. Had you consented to the wish expressed by many of your friends that you should write, out of the fulness of your knowledge and experience, a treatise on the game of polo, I at all events should never have ventured on the task. But even though you have refused the labour, the credit of this book must still be yours, for what knowledge of Polo I have is derived from your precept, and, still more, from your play of the game of which you are a master, and, in its modern form at least, the creator. Should this book take its place on the shelves of polo players beside the writings of "Dooker" and E. D. Miller, it will be a pleasure to me to think that it may recall to the minds of a future generation of players how much you did for the game and how brilliant a practical exponent of your own precepts you were.

Yours sincerely,

THOS. F. DALE.

THE COTTAGE,
    WEST MALLING.
        1897.

CONTENTS.

		PAGE
Preface...		ix
Chap. I.—The Rise and Development of Polo		1
,, II.—The Training of the Player		18
,, III.—The Education of the Pony...		37
,, IV.—The Game		48
,, V.—The Umpire ...		91
,, VI.—Management of the Polo Club		99
,, VII.—Polo in India...		114
,, VIII.—Polo in the Colonies and Abroad ...		128
,, IX.—Polo Ponies ...		133
,, X.—Stable Management and the Wintering of Polo Ponies		149
,, XI.—Pulling Ponies		159
,, XII.—Breeding Polo Ponies and the P.P. Stud Book Society		178
,, XIII.—The Dress and Equipment of the Player ...		186
,, XIV.—The Expense and Danger of Polo ...		190
,, XV.—Polo Clubs		197
,, XVI—Recollections and Reflections		205
Rules of Polo ...		223
Principal Tournaments and Winners		264
List of Clubs ...		269

ILLUSTRATIONS.

Mr. John Watson ... Photogravure... ... ... *Frontispiece.*

FULL-PAGE SEPIA PLATES.

"Nimble" (New Zealand pony) ... ... *Face page*	16
"Gold" ... ... ,, ,,	34
"Dynamite" ... ... ,, ,,	58
"Skittles" ... ... ,, ,,	66
"Johnnie" (Arab) ... ... ,, ,,	86
"Shy Lass" ... ... ,, ,,	100
"Rangoon" (Burmese pony)... ... ... ,, ,,	124
"The Bey" (Arab) ... ... ,, ,,	152
"Boadicea" ... ... ,, ,,	172
"Fitz" ... ... ,, ,,	190
Mr. W. H. Walker's ponies—"Nimble," "Cicely," "Dynamite," "Lady Jane" ... ... ,, ,,	204
"Chance" (New Zealand pony) ... ... ,, ,,	224

ILLUSTRATIONS IN THE TEXT.

	PAGE
Polo in Persia	5
The Game in those days was dangerous	11
The most Brilliant Player	13
"At each Blow the Ball flies"	21
Waiting for a Miss	33
Always to Gallop	36
"As Good as a Bank Note"	38
In a good large Figure of Eight	41
Pushed Clean off his Legs	45
No. 1 Clears the Road	52
No. 2, A Brilliant Run	60
Out of the Game	69
Saved	73
Clearing the Way	85
A Sitting Shot	89
The Chief Danger of Polo	92
Captain Walter Smythe	111
Polo in India	121
Pulling is undoubtedly the worst	160
Turn your Ponies	163
The Standing Martingale	168
Something of a Puller	173
Wrinkling up the corners of his mouth	175
The Action of a Double Bridle	177
The Pavilion at Ranelagh	200
Crooked his Stick in the Air	207
"Stoneclink"	251

PREFACE.

IF it had been necessary to offer an excuse for the writing of this book, the book itself would never have been written. But as Polo is a game which is still in the stage of evolution, there is much to chronicle of the changes which time brings. Even now the chief authorities of the game—the Hurlingham Club—are considering certain changes in the rules which may affect the game in the future.

The present season has indeed seen the greatest alteration of late years. The height of ponies has been fixed at 14·2, and Sir Henry Simpson has been appointed Official Measurer to the Hurlingham Club. This is undoubtedly a great step in the progress of evolving a scientific game out of what at first was no more than a pleasant and friendly pastime. This book is the result of a careful study of the game, first, as an ardent, though never a brilliant player for more than ten years, and then as one whose duty it was to watch most of our chief players when reporting great matches or meditating articles for *Land and Water*, *The Sporting and Dramatic*, *The Field*, *Baily's Magazine*, *The Asian*, and the *Civil and Military Gazette* of Lahore. This

Preface.

is no doubt an excellent training for a sound knowledge of the game; how far I have profited by it is for the following pages to show. To the period during which I filled the place of Polo Manager at Ranelagh I feel I owe much. A Polo Manager who has to make up games, perforce studies the play of the members with great care. But this is not the only benefit he derives, for it is a position which enables him to hear the opinions and profit by the experience of those who are acknowledged masters of the game. In particular I desire here to express my obligations to Captain Walter Smythe, Mr. Gerald Hardy, and Mr. A. Rawlinson, for the kindness with which they have ever given me assistance and information on polo matters. It is impossible not to feel as I read over the pages of this book before it goes to press, how much I owe to the three writers on polo, Messrs. Moray Brown, E. D. Miller, and Captain Younghusband, yet at the same time I alone am responsible for the opinions and precepts I have given. I have striven to make them as far as possible the expression of the experience and knowledge which I have myself acquired during the years in which I have played polo and watched others playing it.

Two objects I have had before me. First, to be of use to those who desire to play the game, and next to make it more interesting to spectators, by enabling them to understand its objects and follow the chances of a match. For as no game is more

Preface.

puzzling to the ordinary spectator than polo, none is more delightful or exciting to those who have grasped the principles of the game.

To the three artists who have illustrated the book, and more particularly to Miss L. C. Smythe, from whose drawings the pictures of ponies are reproduced, the book will owe much of its attractiveness.

To " Trant," the well-known writer on Women's Sport, I owe thanks for assistance in the preparation of the text for the press, at a time when the pressure of other engagements made this necessary work impossible to me.

Lastly, to Mr. C. E. Rose, Royal Horse Guards, at whose suggestion the book was written; to my friend Mr. Tresham Gilbey, who permitted me to use the block of an excellent portrait of Captain Smythe which had appeared in *Baily's Magazine*, to Mr. Adrian Jones and Miss Imogen Collier, who have allowed sketches to be made from drawings of theirs, I offer my grateful acknowledgments.

CHAPTER 1.

THE RISE AND DEVELOPMENT OF POLO.

THE game of polo is one of the oldest, if not quite the very oldest, of all sports which still exist. It goes back indeed to the year B.C. 600, and, so far as we can tell, it seems to have been of Persian origin. The ancient Persians, who, like ourselves, were people of athletic tastes, were especially fond of those games and sports which displayed skill in horsemanship. Polo is a sport which is suitable to a warlike people and is, in itself, almost a military exercise. The qualities which make a man a good cavalry soldier are exactly those which are needed in a good polo player—quickness, dash, decision, and pluck. In those old-world favourites the *Tales of the Thousand and One Nights* we not only find allusions to the game now known as polo, but in the *Tale of the Wazir and Sage Duban* we are told the story of its invention. In "days of yore and images

The Rise and

long gone before" we read that a king, called Yunan, reigned over the city of Fars, of the land of the Roum. This king was afflicted with leprosy which none of his physicians could cure, but at last there came a sage who asked permission to undertake the treatment of the sovereign's case, and promised that he would give neither potion to drink nor ointment to anoint him with. The King graciously gave permission to the unknown to exert his skill on his behalf, and from this point in the quaint story we may follow the translation of the original Arabic as given by Sir Richard Burton.

"Then he," the sage, "set to work at choosing the fittest drugs and simples, and he fashioned a bat, hollow within and furnished with a handle without, for which he made a ball; the two being prepared with consummate art. On the next day, when both were ready for use and wanted nothing more he went up to the King; and kissing the ground between his hands bade him ride forth on the parade ground there to play pall and mall. He—'the King'—was accompanied by his suite, emirs, and chamberlains, wazirs and lords of the realm, etc. Ere he was seated the sage Duban came to him, and handing him the bat said, 'Take this mall and grip it as I do; so! and now push for the plain and leaning well over thy horse drive the ball with all thy might until thy palm be moist and thy body perspire, then the medicine will penetrate through

Development of Polo.

thy palm and will permeate thy person. When thou hast done with playing and thou feelest the effects of the medicine, return to thy palace and make the Ghusl ablution in the Hammam bath, and lay thee down to sleep; so shalt thou become whole, and peace be with thee.'

"Thereupon King Yunan took the bat from the sage and grasped it firmly, then mounting steed he drove the ball before him and galloped after it till he reached it, when he struck it with all his might, his palm gripping the bat handle the while, and he ceased not malling the ball till his hand waxed moist, and his skin, perspiring, imbibed the medicine from the wood."

This shows that the game was regarded as a preventive of ill-health and effeminacy arising from a soft life and want of exercise, and to this day the story may be read and applied by men who are conscious of the mental and physical inertia arising from a too sedentary work or the even more harmful lack of employment altogether. But polo was a long time in reaching England, and until a comparatively recent date was only known in the East. From the Persians the game passed to the Turks, and thence by way of Thibet, Ladakh, and Kashmir to Manipur, where it was and is a national sport. The first Englishmen to play the game were the indigo planters of Bengal, and in that district for some years the game stopped without gaining any

The Rise and

ground in India outside the planting districts. Then so far as can be gathered the game was played in Bengal in an irregular fashion by officers of native cavalry regiments who used their chargers for the purpose. Indeed there is no trace of the game having been played among English officers till after the Mutiny. The Persians undoubtedly used horses for the game, nor was it till polo reached India that ponies were employed, and even these were probably used at first simply because the hill tribes possessed no horses. The fitness and adaptability of the pony for polo was practically an accidental discovery. To the Manipuris then must be conceded the honour of being the immediate forerunners of the polo players of to-day.

The introduction of polo into England was the result of a lucky inspiration of some officers of the 10th Hussars then stationed at Shorncliffe. It is said that their chargers were the mounts, hockey sticks and a billiard ball the implements of these adventurous players. The honour of the introduction, however, is also claimed for the 9th Lancers, who have since engaged in friendly conflict for so many polo trophies with the 10th Hussars. In any case, so quickly did the game commend itself to these two regiments and so great did its possibilities appear that the horses were soon exchanged for ponies, the billiard ball for the willow root ball now in use, and the hockey club for the regular

POLO IN PERSIA.

From an old painting found in the palace of the King of Oudh.

(*Now in the possession of Mr. W. M. Meredith.*)

Development of Polo.

polo stick. The first polo club was the Monmouthshire, founded by Captain Herbert in 1872, and after this polo found a home at the Lillie Bridge grounds. How rapid its rise into favour may be noted from the fact that in 1878 the first Inter-Regimental Tournament was played and won by the 5th Lancers. Nor has this regiment ever received quite the credit due to it in this matter. There can be no doubt that polo had been more or less of a scramble up to the time when the 5th, returning from India, where they had learnt the game, proved themselves the best exponents of play in this country. Then the 7th Hussars came to the fore, and they have always kept up their regimental polo and have held their own in India ever since.

But the great event in the history of English polo was the decision arrived at by the Hurlingham Club to take up the game.

It was reserved for Captain Monson, who had been manager of Hurlingham since 1870, to see the possibilities of the game, and to advise the club committee to make a polo ground. In consequence of this the ground which is now so familiar to all lovers of the game throughout the world was laid out. The Hurlingham ground, it is true, is not a perfect one by any means. A polo ground should be rectangular, and Hurlingham is egg-shaped, and what is perhaps even worse is that there is a considerable fall towards the goal near the chestnuts.

But good management has atoned for these disadvantages, and some of the finest games ever played have been seen upon the beautiful green surface, which is a perfect model of what the *turf* of a polo ground should be. For twenty years and more the ground has been trodden in after each game, and watered and cared for under the superintendence of Captain Smythe and the head gardener, Mr. Sutherland. And if the club was fortunate in having a general manager who was alive to the possibilities of polo in Captain Monson, it was no less lucky in having as its first polo manager, Captain Smythe. Very much of the success of a polo club necessarily depends on its manager or secretary, and all that could be done was done to make Hurlingham Polo a success. The committee had not long to wait to see the success of their new departure, for members flocked in, and the club became not only as fashionable a resort as ever it had been in the heyday of pigeon shooting, but it rapidly became the recognised centre of polo.

The Hurlingham Committee first drew up for polo an authoritative code of rules which have practically been accepted everywhere as the laws of the game. There is no country where polo is played that has not adopted the Hurlingham code as the foundation of its rules, varied only by the special necessities of each club. These Hurlingham rules have been carefully revised lately by the very representative polo

Development of Polo.

committee of the club. As the members of this committee are practical players, they have been able to see not only where new rules were needed, but have made the wording of the former rules much more clear than they were in their original form, and thus done much to prevent disputes in the future. The position of the Hurlingham Committee as the chief authority on polo was one not sought or even desired perhaps by its members. But its authority has increased with the world-wide growth of the popularity of polo, and the committee has perforce accepted the position which the inevitable course of events has forced upon it.

We have, however, got rather beyond the strict sequence of events in the history of polo, for the present code of rules would have been scarcely intelligible to the early players of the game. There was to begin with no fixed number of players in a team, there being seldom fewer than five and sometimes as many as eight. Nor was there any particular order observed; the first germ of the modern system being found in the appointment of a goalkeeper whose duties were to keep near the goal he defended and who seldom or never went up into the game. This player could not have had a particularly exciting time. The one object set before a young player in any place except that of goalkeeper was to keep on the ball and hit it as often as possible. Some teams preserved a

The Rise and

semblance of order by ruling that when the ball was tried at but not struck, the man who missed should wheel round and come in at the end of the line, gradually working his way up as those in front missed in their turn. This had the effect of producing some sort of coherence in the play of a team and ensuring that the players should back one another up and not get in each other's way. But polo as then played could have had but a short popularity. It could have been but the fashion of a season, something a little more exciting than lawn tennis, and a little less scientific than golf. But while the Hurlingham Club was preparing an arena for the game, away in India the great polo reformer, Mr. John Watson, was thinking out the important changes in the game which have made it the sport it is, and have ensured it a lasting place among our national pastimes.

Mr. John Watson was then a subaltern in the 13th Hussars, a regiment which had taken to the game at once, and he quickly reached a high position as a player of skill. But Mr. Watson felt, as I think all who have played the old game must have felt, that though exciting as an exercise, polo was, as a game, wanting in method and opportunities for the exercise of skill. Moreover the game in those days was dangerous, and I have seen more collisions and falls in a week in the old game than could now be witnessed in a season.

Development of Polo.

Moreover the pace was necessarily slow owing to the fact that everyone got in everybody else's way. Many players too used a short-handled cane made rather heavy, and with this they dribbled the ball along. Backhanders were practically unknown, and when a man got hold of a ball lying in dangerous nearness to the goal he proceeded to take it round at once as far as he could. Mr. Watson's

THE GAME IN THOSE DAYS WAS DANGEROUS.

great idea was the backhander, the effect of which was to quicken the game by causing the ball to travel to and fro straight up and down the ground. From this came the first great change in the game and the revolution was striking. Everyone wanted more ponies and more frequent changes, the old ponies were soon out-classed, and handiness was now the first requisite.

The Rise and

About the same time Back was called up into the game and ceased merely to be a goalkeeper. Soon after these changes had been made, Mr. John Watson returned to England, and left the service, and at once he became what he has ever since remained, the first polo player in the United Kingdom. Others, it is true, may be quicker than he, for his weight tells against him, and some men may hit as straight, but no one, to my mind, can place a ball or control a team as well as he. For some fifteen years he has seen the game of which he is the creator in its modern form, improving, and his own pupils taking their place among the most successful players of the day. His influence over both Indian and English polo it would be difficult to exaggerate. His reforms and those which have grown out of them have given to the game pace, order and science.

There is also another consequence which follows from the changes introduced, but this, I imagine, Mr. Watson did not think of. The game is now interesting to watch, for, with but a little attention and experience, the looker-on can tell where each player ought to be, and what he ought to be doing. Now, spectators may not be actually necessary to the enjoyment of players, and they may indeed be rather demoralizing by exciting to gallery play, but they are necessary, or at least useful to the support of the clubs which like Hurlingham and Ranelagh do most for

Development of Polo.

the game, and they certainly afford a stimulus to the players by their interest. I think indeed that no game of the class of polo has much chance of long-lived popularity which fails to interest those who do not play themselves. In any case with polo the critical part of the spectators of the game grows yearly, for each year increasing weight or age, or it may be marriage, removes some fine players from the active to the retired list.

THE MOST BRILLIANT PLAYER.

Valuable, however, as Mr. Watson's services to the game undoubtedly were, there can be no doubt that the exposition of good polo and fine combination shown by the Messrs. Peat and Mr. Mildmay and Lord Harrington, helped greatly to raise the general level of play. Day after day, combined or separate, these fine players, who to great skill added perfect loyalty to their side, and a keen

The Rise and

sense of the value of combination, showed at Hurlingham or at Ranelagh what the game could and should be. To have seen polo at its best outside the regimental teams, it is necessary to have followed the three brothers playing with a man they trusted. It was not that they were all superlatively great players. Mr. J. E. Peat stood out indeed as the most brilliant player of modern times, but the other two brothers though good were not better than other men of the first class. Their strength lay in the fact that they played absolutely with one heart and one will, and that they had each an instinctive perception of what the others could or would do in each particular case. They were players of the most scrupulous fairness, and there never was less disputing than when the brothers were in their glory. They put in practice Mr. Watson's teaching, and while the latter could only show us how to play in one place in a team, the Sussex County team showed how four men could play as one.

I have said that spectators are not altogether an unimportant factor in the popularity of the game, but until recently polo was little known or understood outside the clubs or away from Dublin, where a really fine player was and is a popular idol of the sport-loving Irish.

Polo in those days had no literature. Short and perfunctory paragraphs only recorded the

Development of Polo.

great matches, and these even the most enthusiastic lovers of the game found unreadable. Just at the right moment appeared the man who was needed to give the crowning touch and finish to polo, by making the story of great matches interesting, and the points of the game intelligible to both the on-lookers and readers. James Moray Brown (Dooker) brought to his task knowledge, enthusiasm and a vivid style. So life-like and pictorial were his accounts of polo in tournaments, which like the Inter-Regimental stirred the soldier as well as the sportsman in him, that you could hear as you read the quick recurrent thud of galloping ponies and the crack of stick and ball meeting. Yet Moray Brown was no conscious word-painter. His style was but the reflection of the enthusiasm and keenness of the man. In every part where Englishmen were to be found his polo articles and his reports (in which were his best work) were read. The effect of his writing on the game was very great. He made it interesting and he made it intelligible, and I believe that his writing was directly the cause of the spread of polo in the Colonies. No one but those who have been in exile know how eagerly each part of the home papers is scanned by those far from the interests and pleasures of home. I can well remember the discovery of Moray Brown's first articles on polo in an Indian Station library and the effect they produced on myself, and I can understand that a man carried away by the vivid description and obvious enjoyment of the writer in his subject should desire to experience the pleasure of that "elixir of pace" in polo, of which Dooker loved to write. Alas! our friend stayed with us but a short time after he had discovered his vocation. Weary and worn with work that was heavy and often uncongenial, he had no power to resist the attacks of the fever which killed him. Yet I think that his thoroughness, his straightforwardness, and his kindliness, will not soon be forgotten by this generation of players. I like to fancy that his old friends still miss him from his wonted seat on the top of the pavilion at Hurlingham, and would be glad if they could invoke Dooker's judgment on a polo pony or take his opinion on a knotty point of polo. No history of polo could be complete without a respectful mention of the place of Moray Brown, the first and best writer on polo we have yet had. Other names there are which future writers may speak of as having done something for the game, but they are still working, and the time has not yet come to appraise their work. Yet perhaps we could hardly avoid speaking of Mr. E. D. Miller and his brother, the present polo managers at the Ranelagh Club, who have made as many good players by precept and example, and brought out more good polo ponies than any other men of the day.

New Zealand Pony "NIMBLE." 6 years. (Thoroughbred.)

Development of Polo.

Thus have we followed the course of polo from its first beginning to the present time, and seen how it has grown from being the military exercise of Persian princes or the national sport of an obscure hill-tribe to a game of unsurpassed interest and skill in England, India, and indeed all over the world. In India, the introduction of polo is coincident with the decline of other sports. Pig sticking is not to be had everywhere nor indeed to any good purpose in many places, cricket and football are not well suited to the climate, big game shooting is scarce, and leave is often scarcer still at the best seasons of the year, but polo is always possible and can be played all the year round.

Moreover the game has an advantage over all others, and this is as great in England as elsewhere. It takes up very little time and it is therefore *par excellence* the recreation of busy men. In this country it is true it can never take the place of hunting, but it can and does rival it in the affections of many, and it is of course far cheaper, especially to those men who are in the "Service." The one thing which on looking back over the history of polo it seems to lack is a poet. With the exception of two verses of Oman Khalyam, the game has not yet stirred the imagination of a poet. Persian writers indeed allude to it, but polo has yet to find its Somerville or at any rate its Whyte Melville.

CHAPTER II.

THE TRAINING OF THE PLAYER.

THERE is no game more stirring to watch than first-class polo, and it is probable that many a man after seeing one of our best matches has come away saying to himself, "I, too, will be a polo player." Nor will anyone be likely to doubt the soundness of his decision, for there is no game that combines exercise, excitement and danger in such exact and excellent proportions. Moreover, polo does not take up nearly so much time as cricket or football, nor does it require much more money. It is a popular delusion that polo is an expensive game. In proportion to the pleasure it brings, it is not so, and for the busy man it is probably one of the cheapest forms of recreation, for it gives exercise and health for the smallest possible expenditure of time of which the anxious man of business has probably less to spare than of anything else. There was a time, indeed, not so long ago, when business men were men of affairs and nothing else, and it was then thought to be unbusinesslike and undignified for them to take much share in games. Tennis indeed might be permitted to a city father provided he did not play too well, and badminton,

The Training of the Player.

or "hit and scream," as the irreverent subaltern in India calls it, was considered thoroughly respectable. But we have changed all that. We now wax our mustachios, smoke cigarettes in business hours, and desire some active exercise for the benefit of our health and digestion.

To this end what can possibly be better than polo? But how to become a player? The answer is summed up in two words—Ponies and Practice.

Ponies I put first because not only are they necessary to the game but the player's whole future depends on the kind of pony on which he begins to play. Now it is here and at the very beginning that most men make a mistake. The aspiring player visits a polo ground and presently sees a man dart out with the ball and gallop for the goal, while at each crack the ball flies onward and the pony fairly lays itself down in pursuit. The other players try to catch the leader, but in vain. A neat near side hit under the pony places the ball, and the animal answering to the touch of the rider, twists and turns as the ball shoots to this side or that, till the man gets a fair shot and the ball rising up from the hoof-trodden turf flies well into the air through the posts. Who whoop!

The sight lingers in the mind of the new hand, and when he sees "Kitten, good polo pony, etc., the property of Captain Smith, ordered abroad," etc., etc., and realises that this is the pony he saw

The Training of the Player.

playing in the match about which he has so often dreamed, he goes off to Tattersall's, buys it at a longish price, and then goes home to dream of brilliant runs and successful goals. But when on the following morning he mounts the new purchase and arms himself with a stick and ball, how different is the reality. He finds it impossible to hit the ball twice running, and by the time he has jagged at the Kitten's mouth and hit her on the nose and on the legs once or twice, he finds she is not the easy brilliant mount he had thought her. She begins to fret and twist, and worst of all to pull, and he returns after a quarter of an hour's practice, during which time he has perhaps hit the ball once —with the mare in a lather and a decidedly bad temper, and he himself under the firm conviction that he has been stuck. Not at all. The Kitten is a first-class polo pony. She is fast, handy and keen, but she has been accustomed to a first-rate player on her back, and she has a profound contempt for our novice friend.

Now the pony he ought to have bought, and which he will yet have to buy, if he is ever to learn the game, is a different kind of animal altogether. Somewhere amid that crowd of ponies on the match ground there was probably one that would not catch the eye. A pony with a sober eye and a somewhat dejected aspect, with legs that show wear and tear, and not possessing half the grace and quality of the

"AT EACH BLOW THE BALL FLIES."

The Training of the Player.

Kitten, but all the same, when our novice gets on old Mentor's back, polo will seem quite an easy game by comparison. The old pony knows the game and loves it. True he is somewhat losing his pace, but to make up for this he never shies off the ball; he always knows where it is, and will turn on a sixpence, and this so quickly as to shake the seat of the unwary. I have indeed seen one such old stager fairly go from under his rider and leave him sitting ignominiously on the ground when the ball had flown back from a neat backhander. On the other hand, if you hit his callous old legs or steady yourself by his mouth, his temper will not be thereby upset. He goes after the ball as fast as he can and never pulls, and he will stand, if need be, with I know not what calm contempt in his mind, while the novice makes two or three ineffectual shots at a sitting ball.

This is the beginner's pony, so buy old Mentor if you can get him, and by so doing you will have made a great stride towards becoming a player. The next thing to do is to get a well-balanced stick that suits you. It is impossible for anyone to say exactly how you are to do this, for every man must work the matter out for himself, trying sticks till he finds one of the length, weight and pliability that he requires. Probably for a beginner a stick should be rather heavier than the one he would choose after he has become a more practised player.

The Training of the Player.

Having possessed himself of the pony and the stick, the first thing for the beginner to learn is to hit the ball at a slow pace straight forward and continuously. For this purpose a road is the best place, and if you have a longish drive or know of a good straight stretch of road not too frequented, you had better make use of it. Now drop the ball on the ground and hit it straight in front of you, trying to keep it in motion in as direct a line as possible. I am certain that to begin with no practice can be better than this for giving the power to hit the ball, and also a certain control over it. As soon as a sufficient mastery of the ball has been attained, and the player can drive it straight a-head, hitting it on the near or off side indifferently, it will be time to make another step forward. But the practice should be continued till you have attained a considerable degree of certainty. While you have been doing this you will have incidentally learned some useful lessons, and will, among other things, have decided on the length and weight of stick you require.

Let old Mentor be saddled then, and this time take him with stick and ball into a field, and choosing a fairly level space begin to canter about at a steady pace. Do not go too fast, for the object of these first lessons is to overcome the difficulty of hitting the ball on rough ground, and at first it will be as much as you can do to effect this at a slow

The Training of the Player.

pace. The ball you will find will rise and turn off in the most provoking manner, and it will seem to evade your blows almost with the intelligence of a living thing. The most profitable practice now will be to hit the ball straight forward to a given point, say a white stone or a certain tree, or you may put up two posts at either end of the exercise ground to serve as goal posts. Remember, however, from the first, that it is not sufficient to hit the ball. You must always endeavour to get command of it, and make it go in the direction you wish. It is just this control over the ball, the power to place it, that makes the difference between such players as Messrs. John Watson, E. D. Miller or W. Buckmaster, and those who never come into the front rank. One man is superior to another in polo according as he has the power to place the ball where he will. It is of small use in a game to be able to take the ball down the ground at full speed if you cannot prevent it from turning to one side or the other, or if from the force of the last blow it flies over the boundary line at a considerable distance to one side of the posts.

The control at which you must aim is the result of a good eye, good horsemanship, and much practice, and it is with the last of these that we are now concerned. This seems a good place therefore to say how very necessary to your success constant and regular practice will be. There is no doubt

The Training of the Player.

this is much neglected, but since an imaginary pupil is necessarily obedient, I will picture him each day, mounted on old Mentor, and cantering steadily after the ball in a given direction. It is not a good plan, remember, to ride about a field after a ball without any definite plan in your mind, for though that kind of chance hitting may be of use to the finished player, to whom it will be a benefit to get the ball in a variety of positions, to the beginner it is no good. Let the novice therefore be at first contented to put up his goal posts and ride at a moderate pace from one end of the ground to the other. It is now that the practice of backhanders may come in, and they should be taken on the near and off side as occasion offers. I am aware that, inasmuch as the near side stroke is the more difficult, players are sometimes exhorted to learn to hit on the off side first, but I do not agree with this. If your practice follows the lie of the ball then it will become a habit to do what is required at the moment, and this will be found a great advantage in the game itself. I would therefore have the player set before his mind the task of hitting the ball first through one goal and then through the other, hitting backhanders or near siders as the movements of the ball may require. These will be found of great variety, for even polo grounds are never absolutely level, and in consequence the chances of the game are considerable. That the

The Training of the Player.

uncertainty adds greatly to the interest no one will deny, for it gives to polo the never-ending variety of incident and excitement that makes it so delightful both to play and to watch.

This period of practice will be a long one before the player can hope to gain a reasonable certainty of hitting the ball at all at a moderate pace. As soon, however, as this is attained, the pace must be quickened, and old Mentor must be asked to stretch himself. As he is an animal of experience and prudence, he is not likely to overwork himself. But even a pony of Mentor's virtue will not stand over-much practice, or he will turn cunning and dodgy. Do not therefore give him too much, as I am anxious that you should go into your first game on the pony on which you have been practising, for thus you will have more confidence, and there will be more likelihood of your playing well and remembering the lessons you have learned than if you are mounted on a pony to which you are not accustomed. Therefore since old Mentor can only do a certain amount of work, and you will need more practice than he alone can give you, some other plan must be tried. Now, there is no finer player in India than Major le Lisle, of the Durham Light Infantry, and he has adopted a plan which he finds useful even now, and which I many years ago advocated. It is this. Have a wooden horse made about the size of the polo pony's standard height.

The Training of the Player.

Seat yourself on it, and get someone to bowl a polo ball towards you, and from behind you, while you hit through the goal posts with either a meeting or following stroke. The pony of wood should be placed at various angles to the posts, and this will give you practice in goal-hitting, which is one of the points to which beginners often fail to give sufficient attention. It is a difficult feat, and requires more mastery over the ball than any other stroke in the game, yet is it seldom or never practised. I strongly advocate the striking at a ball bowled towards you, for although to meet a ball is a difficult and risky stroke, and one not to be attempted in the game, except in cases of dire necessity, yet it is capital exercise, and helps to give you quickness and readiness. This practice on the wooden horse is most valuable, and every one who aspires to play polo well should give at least half an hour a day to it.

When you have done all that I have suggested here you will have done much, but, if you are disposed to do more, you might then with advantage look out for another pony, also a steady one and experienced in the game, and go through the whole course again. It will be a great advantage when you can do as well on one pony as the other, and can change from Mentor to the Schoolmarm and back again without much difference in your play.

It is not unlikely that in the course of practice the would-be player will find himself not to be so

The Training of the Player.

good a horseman as he had supposed. For although Englishmen are beyond other nations fond of horses and of those sports in which horses bear a part, yet the number of really good horsemen among them is surprisingly small. The reason of this is that so long as a man can ride straight in a creditable manner across country and does not fall off with little or no provocation, he is satisfied. There are many instances of men who have done well in the hunting field who were, nevertheless, very indifferent horsemen. Nor am I going to say here that horsemanship of the finer kind is necessary for the polo player. I have known many good players who could not be called fine riders. But as I am writing now to those who are beginning the game, I may say that the quality of your horsemanship will make a great deal of difference to your enjoyment of the game, and must make some difference in your play. However good a player a man may be, there can be no question that if he improves in horsemanship he will at the same time become more proficient in the game. Fortunately polo is the best possible school for riding, for it strengthens the seat and gives power and control over the horse to an extent which nothing else can do. If, therefore, the young player finds out that he is not so good a horseman as he could wish, let him, after following out the course I have marked out, add a promising young pony to

The Training of the Player.

his establishment, and proceed to train him for polo. You must not of course use the stick or ball on him until you have sufficient control over these latter to make it unlikely that you will strike him by mistake, but remember that everything you teach the pony will at the same time improve your own seat and hands. The rider who follows out concurrently with his own practice the training of a polo pony will start in the game with a distinct advantage.

Let us suppose then that the beginner has profited by his own training, that he has a fair certainty of hitting the ball and has even some control over its direction when not going too fast, and that he can hit a fair backhander. It now remains to learn to gallop and to play the game, and this can only be done on the ground and with other players. So there is nothing for it but to send on the two ponies to the polo ground of the club to which you belong and there measure your skill with others. If you really wish to be in the front rank of players work at a local or county club only will not be sufficient for you. You must play also at one of the great polo centres, at Hurlingham, Ranelagh, or Rugby. Indeed I should strongly recommend any keen beginner to try to join one of these large clubs. If he goes to the ground early in the season and takes care to be in good time he will get plenty of practice and very likely in the best of company.

The Training of the Player.

Up to this time I have been advising the young player not to go beyond the pace at which he can retain a due mastery over the ball, but once you are in the game I should say now give all your mind to riding. Ride hard and never disturb yourself about missing. Above all things keep galloping. Polo is much more than hitting the ball, and when you find yourself in a game your first duty is absolute loyalty to your side. For polo has now become rather a game of combination than one which calls for the display of individual prowess, and you have to take your place as one of four players animated by a unity of purpose. From the first make up your mind to do your best in every game. Do not say "It is only a members' game," or that you "want to save your ponies." If the latter indeed be an object the animals will be better off in their stable than spoiling both your own and other peoples' play. In whatever place you find yourself do your best to keep it and strive to do the greatest possible service to your side. As you become more accustomed to the game it is true you will find that you can do better in one place than another, and then you will more often than not find the sides so arranged that you may be in the place that suits you best. At first, however, you need not trouble yourself about this, for it is of great importance that every player should learn to be useful everywhere. But wherever you find yourself, study the play of

The Training of the Player.

others and learn their peculiarities, so that you may be able to take advantage of the weaknesses of your adversaries or supplement those of your friends as occasion may require. If you become acquainted with the play of others you will then be able to fit into any place when taking part in a members' game.

There are certain faults that are very common and should be guarded against. For example, you may often see a man hanging back instead of riding up to an adversary because he hopes or thinks the latter will miss the ball, and he expects to turn on it and get a clear run. This should never be. Always go right up and hustle. If there is a miss the man behind you on your own side will, if he is worth anything, get the ball. It is true you will not get the run, will not indeed hit the ball, but to get runs is not the chief aim of polo, and you have to consider not what will bring you most prominently forward, but what will be the best for your side. When it is your duty to ride a man off always go right up to him and hustle. Do not make little spurts and never go right in. Remember always to get alongside the adversary and endeavour to hustle him off. Stick to your opponent. In a first-class game you will occasionally see the whole eight players race down on the ball in pairs, riding so close that for any one of them to hit the ball is impossible.

Always be ready to leave the ball if you note

WAITING FOR A MISS.

"GOLD."

THE PROPERTY OF SIR HUMPHRY DE TRAFFORD, BART.

The Training of the Player.

that it is better placed for one of your own side than for yourself, and it will be well to leave it if the man behind you is in his place, and you can clear the way by riding off another player. Whenever a player of known reputation is inclined to give you hints listen and obey. Do not, however, leave off practice as soon as you begin to play. On the contrary, you should get some practice every day if possible, for it is now that you will find out your weak points, and these can best be corrected in private. Your course of solitary play, too, may be extended. I have already advised that before actually going into the game the novice should learn to hit straight forward and back, and to this, after he has begun to play, may be added the practice of taking the ball round in circles. You must also learn to hit across a pony's front and underneath him, indeed, the more directions in which with accurate aim you can hit the ball, the better player you will be. Moreover, though backhanders are the right game, yet there are times when the ball should be taken round. It is not, for example, advisable when you have space before you and a quick pony under you to hit the ball right back into your adversaries' power. But at first "taking round" should be confined to your private practice, as it requires considerable knowledge of the game as well as good judgment to know when such a course is advisable.

The Training of the Player.

A golden rule to remember is to play as much as you possibly can. I have said nothing about preparing yourself for any special place in the game because this is not a point on which you can have general advice. You will find out gradually where you are most useful, and in this something will depend on your temperament and a good deal on the ponies you ride. At first, as I have said before, take any place that may be offered to you and do the very best in it you can. But wherever you are, remember always to *gallop*, for a slow sticky player can never be of any use.

ALWAYS TO GALLOP.

CHAPTER III.

THE EDUCATION OF THE PONY.

THE education of the pony naturally follows that of the training of the player. For though it is true that the pony on which we learn must have been previously schooled, since as we have seen no player can possibly learn quickly on a raw animal, yet, as soon as the player has learned his part, the choice and training of his ponies becomes of the first importance to his success in the game. It is in fact of vital importance, for while a good player will show his best form on a really good polo pony, he will be quite unable to attain to the same style on an inferior animal.

Now there are two ways in which you can provide yourself with first-class ponies. The first is by buying such ready-made animals whenever they come into the market. This is perhaps the most certain and in the end the most economical plan if you can stand the first outlay. For if you buy well-known ponies with an established reputation, take care of them and do not spoil them, they will always fetch their price, and are, as a certain good player always says of his own, "as good as a bank note." To buy the best then is the cheapest in the

The Education of the Pony.

end, and it is also the pleasantest way *for most;* for there is no enjoyment to be had either in hunting or polo unless you are on the best of terms with the animal you ride. There is no greater mistake than to be always chopping and changing, for when you are once suited it is well to recollect that you then have in your possession what money only can never buy—real pleasure and enjoyment. To purchase

"AS GOOD AS A BANK NOTE."

the best ponies then as they come into the market is the best and quickest plan, but to procure four ponies of this class it will cost you not less say than £1,200, and it may be a little more.

Not all of us, perhaps not many, can afford to do this, and the next best plan is to go to the two or three gentlemen who make more or less a regular business of the purchase, training and sale of polo ponies, and who sell annually. The Messrs.

The Education of the Pony.

Miller, of Springhill, Mr. Muriel, of Three Bridges, Mr. Gouldsmith, of Kemble, will probably be able to find you something good at prices which will naturally depend on the quality of the article supplied.

If, however, this plan be in its turn voted too dear, and you have or think you have the gifts of horsemanship required for the task, then buy and train your own ponies. The great examples of success in this line are the Messrs. Peat, Lord Harrington, and Mr. Miller. These players have all been in the habit of buying or breeding their own ponies and putting them through a course of training which has certainly been most successful. Let us suppose then that some men will not only be possessed of the requisite skill, but will enjoy the training of their own ponies. Provided indeed you have the two requirements—SKILL AND LEISURE— you will find no pleasanter task. But if you have not the time or are not willing to make it by deducting it from other pleasure, and if you have not a good stock of patience, a good seat and fair hands, then will you find but little pleasure and less profit in the employment.

First of all the pony must be procured, and advice on this subject will be found in the chapter devoted to polo ponies. Here we have to do with the education of the animal you already have in your stalls. Suppose then that the pony is bought and that he

The Education of the Pony.

or she is quiet in saddle and has a fair mouth and tolerable manners and disposition. Without these natural qualifications, I may say at once the animal has no business in a polo pony stable at all. The first thing now to be done is to make friends with your new purchase and for you to get used to one another. This will be best done by hacking the pony about and getting him used to all sights and sounds, and to waiting patiently while you get on and off. These preliminary excursions together will give you time to learn his peculiarities, if he has any, and to humour or correct them as the case may be. It is no bad plan on such occasions always to carry a polo stick, being careful, however, never to use it in these early days as an instrument of correction. As soon as you are on good terms with one another, begin to canter the pony steadily in a good large figure of eight, taking care that the curves shall be wide and the direction changed till the pony turns as readily in one direction as the other. This result may possibly take some time to accomplish, but it is absolutely necessary to your future success in the field. It is common enough to find ponies that will only turn readily to one side, but it is hardly necessary to point out that this is a grave fault. A polo pony cannot be too handy, and if a choice had to be made between perfect handiness and moderate speed on the one hand, and moderate handiness and great speed on the other, a wise

The Education of the Pony.

choice would incline to the former. A pony cannot be too handy for polo, nor to insure this is there any exercise so good as the figure of eight. It is easy to manage too, and the size of the curves can be perfectly regulated, while to the bending course

IN A GOOD LARGE FIGURE OF EIGHT.

as a method of training there are objections. The latter, indeed, while an excellent test of a pony's handiness at a show and a very pretty and popular exhibition at a Gymkhana, is not by any means the best training for raw ponies. The great thing

The Education of the Pony.

against it is that the bending course is apt to upset the ponies' tempers and to cause the riders to jog their mouths about unnecessarily, unless, indeed, the latter are unusually fine horsemen, and for the benefit of such instructions are not written. At all events the figure of eight is the simplest and best plan and will do all that is required in the preliminary training of a pony.

It should however be remembered that no exercise must be continued long enough to weary the pony. A quarter of an hour before going to his stable will be quite sufficient. Directly he can be turned and twisted easily in large or small circles the lesson may be varied by exercises with the stick and ball. Soon after this kind of practice has begun you will know whether you have a really first-class pony or not. Some animals show a great delight in the game and seem to enter into it from the first, while others as obviously dislike it however carefully they are trained. It is scarcely necessary to say that the former will be more likely to make good polo ponies than the latter.

A point of great importance to be noted in the early training of polo ponies is that they should never be allowed to be above themselves. If a pony has for any reason been in the stable for twenty-four hours or more, take him out for a steady walk and trot for ten miles or so, five miles out and in before you begin your schooling. For if

The Education of the Pony.

it is true that mischief is found for idle hands equally true is it of idle hoofs. Many equine vices are simply exuberant spirits crystallised into habits, and prevention is in such cases very much better than cure. It should be borne in mind that other things being equal steady exercise is the foundation of good manners.

As soon as a pony gallops freely after the ball and you can get him to stretch himself out for a run I would stop this part of his training and go back to figures of eight, circles right and left, and so on. He will thus learn all that is wanted in the game and is not likely to get sick of it before he is actually brought into play. A little trotting and cantering about with the ball just for your own sake is all that will be required henceforth, so far as his actual schooling goes.

Yet is there still an important part of his training to be thought of, for he must be taught to face other ponies and to stand unmoved a good deal of bumping and hustling. Most ponies have no experience of this till they actually go into a game. This is wrong. If a pony is taken into a game and knocked and bumped and hustled till he gets frightened and nervous he is almost certain to contract a dislike and dread of the rough sport. As soon then as the new pony is fairly handy and steady with stick and ball let him be taken out into the field where his stable companions are being

The Education of the Pony.

cantered about, and let them all—I will suppose you have four—canter round and across each other. The riders should be armed with a stick and let there be three or four balls at which to strike. Thus let the ponies pass and re-pass, meeting one another and circling round till they do this without shirking or dodging. Then let two riders start side by side, each armed with a stick and ball, and race up the ground, keeping the ponies close together and letting the young one get his head in front as they near the goal. After this place a ball in the middle of the ground and start the ponies to race for it, the riders jostling and hustling and bumping as they would do in the real struggle. Let the rider of the trained pony pull off a little as the ball is reached and let the youngster and his rider take it on by themselves. Bear in mind that the bumping and jostling should be increased day by day till you find that the pony enters into the spirit of the thing and begins to push and jostle of his own accord just as an American cow pony learns to push and keep his legs as he does so. The Maharajah of Jodhpur's ponies are regularly tested for courage in this way. His plan with a new batch of Arabs is to put light boys up and run them home down the last three furlongs of the race track jostling and pushing as they go. If a pony shows the white feather in these trials he is drafted at once. The capacity for jostling on his own account and for keeping his legs at the same

The Education of the Pony.

time is most necessary for ponies in India, where the rider is not allowed to hustle with his own person, but only to push the pony of the adversary with his mount. A cowardly pony may thus easily be driven over the ball and an unaccustomed one pushed clean off his legs. So clever however do the

PUSHED CLEAN OFF HIS LEGS.

ponies become after such training as I have described that I have seen light Arabs ridden by slight native men stand up and even get the better in a hustle with heavier walers or large Arabs. This point of teaching the pony to hustle is more important with us than it used to be, since the tendency of modern polo rules

The Education of the Pony.

in England is to curtail the liberty of the man to hustle.

The last step in the pony's education is to take him into the game itself, and here I must give counsel which is apparently somewhat adverse to what I have already given in the chapter on the training of the player. For while the man should learn to do his best and work his hardest in every game he plays, the pony should have an easy time at first. Be careful never to ride your pony quite out at first, and remember that a resolute player can get to the bottom of a good polo pony in ten minutes. On the other hand, I dislike pottering play for both pony and rider. But when you take a pony into the game, if he has been thoroughly prepared as suggested above, he will be in good condition and therefore able to gallop and be hustled for five minutes without getting blown, and it will be much better to play him thoroughly in a galloping game for a short time than merely to canter him about for a longer period. If a pony plays well—provided always he is in good condition—he will be able in a week or ten days to take his turn with the others in the ordinary members' games, and at the end of a month should be fit to play in a tournament.

If your ponies are wintered out the same process of training, only shortened, should be gone through before each recurring season, and the polo pony

The Education of the Pony.

should have a day's schooling in turning and bending from time to time throughout the season. This however will not be necessary if the player practices two or three times a week himself, as the pony will thus naturally get his share of the exercise and will gradually improve with his master. There is this, however, to be remembered, that a good pony will become really good in the game much more quickly than his rider will become a good player. If after the early stages then the owner does not seem to himself to be quite up to the mark of finishing the education of a first-class pony in the best way, I would strongly advise him to send the pony to a good player for a short time. If, however, the owner is himself capable of finishing the pony he cannot do better than keep the matter in his own hands, as then and then only the complete unity between man and horse which is so desirable will be preserved.

CHAPTER IV.

THE GAME.

THOUGH several writers of great knowledge and much practical experience have taken in hand the task of giving directions how to play the game of polo, not one of them has been wholly successful. The failure indeed is to be attributed rather to the nature of the subject than to any deficiency of the writers, for it will at once be acknowledged that for a thorough practical and theoretical knowledge of polo, Mr. E. D. Miller and Mr. Moray Brown respectively had the very highest qualifications for guiding the young beginner. Yet most will be equally ready to allow that the directions of neither writer are complete from the novice's point of view, and where such authorities have failed I cannot hope to be more successful. The question, however, cannot be shirked, and even with failure before me I must e'en do my best in offering suggestions to those who are anxious to learn.

Polo, then, it may be conceded, is an essentially difficult game for which to lay down rules of play. There are many and various influences which make all calculations uncertain, and not the least of these is the character of the ground devoted to the sport,

The Game.

for this must necessarily affect all play. In England we have grounds which vary in size and shape and to a very great extent in the quality of the turf with which they are laid. In India, on the other hand, nearly all grounds are alike. They are full-sized, and though somewhat lumpy in places where they are laid with grass, they are hard and very quick, and in consequence the ball is more in the air than it is in England. Thus there the conditions of the game are less variable than they are in this country. Though the difficulties that confront a writer on polo are such as to make it impossible for him to lay down rules to the successful carrying out of which the beginner may pin his faith, it is doubtless one of the charms of the game that it is so impossible to construct a theory of play, or to lay down rules for those who engage in it. Its very chances and uncertainties are among its chief merits, and the game of polo, like the game of life, is so absorbing in its interest, because no one can predict what the future may have in store. There is no game that gives more scope for quick decision as to what is the right thing to do at the moment. No time can be wasted at polo in thinking. The act and thought must work together like the hand and eye of a racket player. Perhaps it is because of this training in rapid decision that good polo players are so successful as masters of hounds. For that this is the case anyone can prove who will run his eye

The Game.

over the field list of hounds and their masters. First among polo players and in the front rank of M.F.H.'s will be found Mr. John Watson, Lord Harrington, Mr. G. Hardy, and Lord Longford, and I might add Mr. Robert Watson, though the last was a master of hounds before he was a polo player.

The game of polo, then, is essentially a game which requires rapid decision in taking advantage of situations that cannot be forecast; but at the same time, for those who wish to learn the rudiments of play, it is no doubt possible to lay down certain regulations of general application. This, then, I propose to do by taking first the duties of each individual player, and then considering the rules to be observed by the team as a whole. I cannot, however, too firmly impress upon those who wish to learn that no hard-and-fast precepts can be given, but that all players who desire to rise to the first rank must mix their obedience to the general laws of play with a goodly proportion of brains.

Let us, then, begin at the beginning, and suppose that a player, being a good horseman and well mounted, and being at the same time not so sure a hitter as some others, occupies the post of Number One. The two leading principles of his play must be to impede the Back of the opposite side and to efface himself when necessary in favour of his own Number Two. In carrying out the first of these

The Game.

duties he will need both the qualifications of which I have already spoken, viz., good horsemanship and a first-rate pony under him. If he has not the former he will continually find himself at a disadvantage. A clever Back—and most Backs are clever, or they would not be in that place, at any rate in a match—will be continually putting an unskilful Number One off side, or otherwise giving him the slip; and the net result of much twisting and turning will be that the latter will ride off the ground feeling the position is a very unsatisfactory one, and that for those who play Number One polo is not so good a game as men say.

On the other hand, he may reflect that he has failed to be of much use to his side, and consider how he could have done more. Now, it is all very well to say—as his Back certainly will say—that it is his duty to ride off the enemy's Back; but to do this in such a way as to clear the road for his own side and prevent the Back from hitting the ball, he must be close to his opponent. Therefore Number One must, above all things, be a good horseman, and he should, moreover, have a cool head. In addition to this, he must be mounted on ponies which should be as fast as possible, and above all must be handy. Nor does the term "handy" mean only that they turn readily, for every pony ridden by Number One must be ready to spring forward and get into his stride at the slightest possible suggestion

The Game.

from his rider. The Back opposed to him will often enough be a heavy man and have decidedly the advantage of weight, and he will also to a certainty be well mounted. Then both Number One and his pony must be bold and indifferent to knocks. For it is no easy matter to ride up to a heavy man who

NO. 1 CLEARS THE ROAD.

is going a good pace on a fast pony and hustle him in such a way as to interfere with his chance of hitting the ball, and especially to prevent him from hitting a backhander.

The best position for Number One to keep is to ride as nearly as possible with his pony's head level with the knee of the Back opposed to him, and

The Game.

then, when he is sure of the direction of the coming stroke, to close with Back and try to bump him off the ball, and thus either clear the way for his own Number Two, or at all events prevent Back from hitting a fair backhander. It is no uncommon fault for a player to shirk the encounter with the Back, and, after riding up full of valour——to do nothing. The good Number One should be as full of resolution and pluck as he is quick and brilliant. This haunting of the Back is his first and perpetual duty, and, while keeping so far behind that he shall not be put off side, he must yet be so near that he can close directly he sees what the Back proposes to do. The obligation is the same whatever Back is doing; and if the latter sees an opening and goes up into the game, Number One should go with him and try to stop the run.

Then I think that Number One's great aim should be to keep the pace as fast as possible. Even the best players like to steady slightly in a run, and thus endeavour to ensure the control of the ball, and Number One can do much by preventing this on the part of the opposing Back. Now, if our Number One be attached to a Back who is fond of going through and up into the game, it is then that he will have some of his best and brightest moments, for of all the thrilling situations of polo that of racing to stop a good player from crowning a brilliant dash with a goal is quite

The Game.

the most exciting next to that of making a run yourself.

The ideal Number. One would be the man who would never allow the opposing Back to hit a backhander or to complete a run, and the nearer he comes up to this standard the better will he be. So far it will be noted that I have said nothing about Number One hitting the ball, and this is just one of those points about which it is difficult to lay down the law, for it is here that the judgment of the individual player must come in. It may be assumed that no one now-a-days would advocate the old plan of a Number One who should never hit the ball at all, and who might be—and sometimes was—sent into the game without even a stick in his hand. Perhaps the best way will be to suggest some occasions when Number One should *not* think first or chiefly of hitting the ball. Thus he should not hit the ball when he can clear the way for either Number Two or Three on his side by hustling the enemy's Back out of the road, or when he can prevent Back from hitting a backhander. To put it generally, it is far more important that he should hinder Back from hitting than that he himself should make a successful stroke. It is seldom indeed that Number One gets a run on the ball, and when he does it is generally an undeserved reward for being where he should not be. There is no worse misdemeanour

The Game.

for Number One than to hang back on the chance of getting the ball if Back should miss it. He should, on the contrary, always go up.

There are, however, two cases in which Number One must hit if he can—the one when he can obviously make a goal, and the other when Back is running the ball and he on a swifter pony has passed him and has a chance of a backhander. Unselfishness is a grace in all polo players; it is a duty in Number One, and perhaps because unselfishness is a somewhat rare quality, the position of Number One is not popular. There are few players who have laid themselves out, so to speak, to become necessary in that position, yet it is probably the most direct way to ensure a young player being selected early to play in good matches as really effective forwards are rare. When such are found it is generally in a regimental team, where discipline and *esprit de corps* over-ride the natural man to a great extent. Nevertheless, the position has its own pleasures, which are, in my opinion, generally underrated, and I would counsel a young player who has a stout heart, light hands, and good ponies to try and make himself master of the duties of Number One. If indeed the glory of a position is in proportion to its responsibility and difficulty then should the reputation of a good Number One stand very high indeed.

Not a few men look on playing Number One in

The Game.

a members' game as an off time for themselves and their ponies. There can be no greater mistake. In whatever position you are placed, whether it be in a match or in the veriest duffers' scramble into which you may be put by the chance of the slate, ride your hardest, hit your straightest, and play the scientific game as thoroughly as though the Inter-Regimental Cup or the Open Championship were to be your reward.

But if, take it all round, the position of Number One of a side is good there can be no doubt that the post held by Number Two is enviable. It is indeed arduous and full of responsibility, but it is brimful of interest and excitement. Number Two also has a simpler task than anyone else in the game, as it is nearly always easy for him to see what he ought to do, and all that remains therefore is to do it as successfully and as thoroughly as he is able. But all the same, this is not a light matter; for to be a good Number Two means good ponies, sure hitting, and great dash. For while Number One may be a good hitter, Number Two *must* be, or he will be of no use to his side. It is Number Two who will most often make the brilliant runs, and to him, probably oftener than to any other member of the team, will be given the applause of the pavilion. For Number Two's duties being the most obvious are consequently the best understood by the spectators. Yet a Number Two whose heart is in his

The Game.

work will be restrained from undue exaltation by a sense of his own shortcomings. A brilliant run is a delightful thing no doubt; but if at the end the ball misses the posts, all the joy of the eager gallop is lost in the sense of failure. "The ground is very bumpy and cut up near the goal, and the ball twisted" is what Number Two says to sympathising friends when he goes off the ground to change ponies, but in his heart he knows he was flurried, that his stick turned a little in his hand, that he had perhaps for the last two strokes lost control of the ball, and that while he could and did hit hard and hit often he did not really take aim at the goal.

The aspiring Number Two is the man of all others who needs practice. His stick must often be in his hand, and for at least five minutes every day—the pace forbids more—he must learn, when going at speed, to hit the ball at or near a mark. There is, remember, much judgment required to make a good and successful run, and the player—and this of course applies to all positions in the game—should be a judge of pace. For the force with which you hit the ball when running for goal should be proportioned to the capability of your pony to get up to the ball while it is still going. If you were playing by yourself this would not matter; but you have an adversary to consider, and one who will probably not be slow to take advantage of the slightest evidence of weakness on your part. If,

The Game.

for example, you hit the ball too hard to the front when your Number One is engaged in riding off the Back, and Number Three of the opposite side is able to pass you in the race for the ball, it is plain that your chance will be gone for the time; but if you only hit to such a distance that you can reach it with your foe hanging on your near side, you will be able to hit again. Thus, if you are galloping on the ball with a very good Number Three, try to keep him on your near side by hitting the ball rather to the right, and then, when you reach it—provided you are ahead of him—if you hit the ball across your front to the left under the pony's neck and swing to the left as you do so, you will obviously still be between Number Three and the ball; and if the Back is well hustled, and you have judged your distance aright, you should have a good chance of hitting a goal. Of course you will often find your enemy on the off side, and then you will have a near side stroke to make; but although you should practice both these strokes diligently, yet the aim of Number Two's tactics should always be to get right-handed strokes straight in front. With regard to the pony's pace, you must study his capabilities and your own to a nicety; but provided you can sit still and hit when the pony is racing under you, you cannot well have too fast a pony, and of course if you have a real flier you can hit as hard to the front as you like, only taking care to reach the ball while

New Zealand Pony "DYNAMITE."
THE PROPERTY OF MR. G. W. SHARMAN.

The Game.

it is still moving, for a moving ball is much easier to control and direct than a dead one. When you have a clear run, and are going down the centre of the ground straight for the goal, it is well to resist all temptations to turn your head. At such times you will often see players, and good ones too, glance over the shoulder, and then if no one is very near, take a pull. I am, however, convinced that this is wrong. You should neither look back—if a faster adversary is near enough to overtake you you will know it soon enough—nor should you steady your pony. Both actions lead to misses. If you are going fast you are more likely to get accuracy of aim and control of the ball if you keep on at the same rate at which you were going before.

It is therefore not enough to ride hard and hit the ball; and if you would have a lesson as to what Number Two should *not* be, watch a few members' games at your club, and it will not be long before you see some dashing, bull-headed player who seldom misses, but who is just as well pleased if the ball goes out over the corner as if he had hit a goal. Such players as these often wonder why the judicious and discerning captains omit to select them for matches. Are they not well mounted? Do they not hit the ball every time they get a chance? And yet, strangely enough, there is no place for them in the match team.

The aim, then, of Number Two is to hit the ball

The Game.

straight to the front whenever there is a chance of doing so. There are, however, certain contingencies of frequent occurrence which modify his duties. If, for instance, the Back of the other

NO. 2. A BRILLIANT RUN.

side is not very certain, or, on the other hand, if his own Number One is a sure hitter, he will need sometimes to efface himself and to be ready when his "first forward" is well on the ball to get

The Game.

to the opposite Back and occupy him so as to give his leader a chance. Under all circumstances Number Two must remember that if his Number One is on the ball and he himself is coming up from behind, that he is not to shout "Leave it" unless he can see a clear advantage for his side to be gained by so doing. He has a choice of two courses: he may either call to the forward to "leave it" or he may get on to the Back, and allow his own man to carry on the ball. This is a matter which each player must decide for himself according to the many and various contingencies which will arise in the course of the game.

Another point which is of great importance is to decide when it is better to leave the ball for Number Three of your own side. This, however, will be determined for you by the quality of the Number Three against whom you are riding. If that player is a good one you will often find your whole energies occupied in holding him and hustling, or in being hustled yourself, and then you must perforce leave the ball to those behind or put it on to the man in front. It may be stated, however, as a general rule, that when the Back in a good team has the ball and is coming up with it, the energies of the three men in front should be concentrated on the duty of clearing the way for that player. For Back is, or should be, the most certain player in a team, and he must be depended upon and trusted. He is, too, the player

The Game.

of most experience, and his judgment as to the best course should be accepted, and, beside this, he is generally a heavy man and well mounted on stout ponies, and his weight and strength will help to carry him through.

Number Two must, then, be a certain hitter, and must have fast ponies and the dash to ride them out. He must also be able to hit on both sides, and to calculate on the effect of a stroke off the boards. I know that some people do not consider play off the boards is sound polo, but with this view I cannot agree. The boards are there; they affect the game, and must, therefore, be taken into consideration. They are, indeed, analogous to the cushions of a billiard table, and should be calculated for in the play. Yet, in this case as in others, it must be borne in mind that the analogy must not be pushed too far. But it is plain that when the pressure of the opposing players is driving the ball across the ground it is better to endeavour to get a stroke off the boards deliberately than to allow the ball to go scuffling along parallel to them. The former will give the players a better chance and improve the game by restoring the battlefield to the middle of the ground.

Of course these tactics are not confined to Number Two, but it will be to him that the chance will most often be given of trying his hand at such strokes. Therefore he should deliberately study the effect of

The Game.

them in members' games, and learn to take advantage of the opportunities thus afforded him. It is one of the duties of Number Two to do his utmost to keep the ball near the middle of the ground when his side is attacking, for clearly the attacking side will have a better chance of making a goal when the ball travels in the direction of the posts from somewhere near the centre of the ground.

When the ball is hit behind the goal line by his own side, and the opposing Back or Number Three is bringing it out, then on Number Two first devolves the duty of preventing the ball from getting back. A great deal depends on this of course, for many goals are made after the ball has been hit out and has by good play on the attacking side been kept near the goal. There are many chances of hitting a goal in such cases, and, besides, a good side often gets demoralised and nervous by the continual nearness of the ball to the goal; and a kind of feeling comes over the defenders that defeat must come—and fear, like prophecy, often brings about its own fulfilment.

For such opportunities as may occur under these circumstances Number Two must be on the lookout. To keep himself steady and cool is his first duty, for many a goal has been missed by flurry or nervousness on the part of Number Two, the player who in most cases has the chance. During these exciting moments his eye must never be off the ball;

The Game.

and amid the scrimmages that will happen he must watch for every opportunity. But fancy shots should not as a rule be attempted, for an inglorious certainty is better than a brilliant chance. When the latter comes off, it is true, it will be greeted with rapturous applause; but it is as well to remember that when it fails, as such shots often do, the feelings of the player will not be enviable.

But when the ball is away flying towards his own goal then must Number Two strive hard to get in front of the opposing Number Three, yet with his pony always well in hand; so that when at length his own Back stops the charge, and the ball comes back again in his direction, he can turn quicker than his immediate adversary and be ready to change defence into attack before the other man can get on to it.

Number Two is no doubt a delightful post, for many will be the runs the player will get; often will he enjoy the excitement of racing for the ball, and not seldom will come the breathless moments when he will be in the midst of the confused mêlée of heads, heels, and sticks from which it is doubtful on which side the ball will come out. But though Number Two is a good position to hold, yet is it a tiring one, and for it the best condition both of man and pony is needed. If either fail he will tire the other; so that for even moderately-successful play the pony must be well exercised, and the man must

The Game.

keep himself in steady resolute training. Late nights, long cigars, and big dinners must be enjoyed but sparingly, for in this as in other athletic sports a not inconsiderable amount of self-denial is necessary before success can be yours.

The judicious captain when arranging a side will probably have but little doubt as to the players whom he should place as forwards, but when it comes to deciding which of the remaining men shall play Three and which Back he will have to pause. The first impulse of many would be to put the best and most trustworthy player as Back, yet it may be an open question whether the most certain hitter and most experienced man should not be placed Number Three. These, at any rate, are the two places in the game which will naturally be filled by the older and more experienced players, and it was of the back players no doubt that Mr. Miller was thinking when he put forth his now celebrated saying that polo was a game for middle-aged men. Assuming then that the choice lies between two players of experience I should be inclined to put the quicker of the two as Number Three, or if there were no difference between them in this respect then to put the more certain man in that position. For Number Three is the man-of-all-work of the team and it will be his duty to hustle and ride off, to attack the adversaries' goal, and to defend his own in turn. But if we endeavour to reduce the

The Game.

duties of Number Three to their first principles by supposing that each man of his side is perfect in his own place, then two objects remain for him to aim at, viz., to ride off Number Two on the other side so as to hinder him from effective attacks, and to pass the ball on to his own forwards and place it so that they can hit it to the best advantage. With regard to the ball it is not the primary duty of Number Three to drive it through the posts but to place it so that his forwards can do so.

When all is going well then these two objects are the first at which Number Three should aim. But the course of polo, like that of true love, never does run smooth, and if the game—in either case—is worth playing at all then Number Three will find that he is expected and obliged to fill up the deficiencies of the other three players. Is Number Two a brilliant but uncertain player then Number Three must back him up and be ready to swoop on the ball when his forward drops it, as perhaps he will do often if it is not his day. Or if, as may well happen, the opposing Number Three is too good for his Number Two, then he must be ready to shout "leave it," and carry out the attack to which that player is unequal. Or again, it may be Number One who is not quite up to his work, willing to ride, but not too bold when hustling is required, or perhaps he is baffled by a smart Back, and is getting out of place and is playing wildly, then there must be a call on

"*SKITTLES.*"

THE PROPERTY OF CAPTAIN D. ST. GEORGE DALY.

The Game.

Number Three to go on to the Back and lead the attack himself. The shout of "off side" coming from his front will be the call to him to go up. Number Three indeed has the right to speak up only second to Back, and he must be ready and able to take the responsibility of doing so whenever it is necessary.

On the other hand when defence is the duty of his side, his eye must be on his own Back—not so impossible really as it looks on paper—and he must be ready to supply his deficiencies or correct his mistakes. In some cases he may find himself protecting the goal or he may dash past Back to save the goal when the latter has missed his stroke. Whether in attack or defence, whatever he is doing, Number Three must never get out of touch with the opposing Number Two, nor must he on any consideration allow that player to go free. Of course his line of action will be modified by his knowledge of the other players. For instance, if he has a first-class Number Two against him he will be specially on his guard lest that player should slip him, but if Number Two is not so good and his own Back is weak or not playing up to his usual form, then he may devote the greater part of his attention to supplementing the deficiencies of his own side.

No part of his duties will require greater attention than the consideration of the occasions when it will

The Game.

be his duty to drop back. Suppose that Back, for instance, has met the ball, a risky play, but like all risks often tempting and sometimes justified by success, or that he has stopped the ball and turned on it, suppose too that Back is a very brilliant player with a fondness on such occasions for running up into the game, then Number Three must without a moment's hesitation drop back into the vacant place. I remember seeing a game in which Three was generally doing Back's duties, and the Back was mostly acting Three or sometimes Two. Both the men were brilliant players, but the loyalty, quickness and certainty with which Three played Back, struck me with more admiration than the good forward play of the man who should have been goal-keeping. But both men were of that class which is to a certain extent independent of or above rules, and therefore do not come under our criticism here. Not so, however, the beginner. He must learn to be content at first to play with as close adherence to rule as is possible.

It is then quite plain that Number Three's worst fault would be to be out of the game. He must indeed always be in the thick of it, and never allow any of the chances and changes to find him galloping by himself. A scattered team, remember, is a beaten team, unless they can pull themselves together in time, and to Number Three belongs the chance of doing this. In such a case he can, as it

The Game.

were, play by himself for a few moments while his forwards are collecting their scattered wits, and while Back gets in front of goal. Even the best teams will sometimes go to pieces suddenly in the most unaccountable manner, and when they do so it will often be the fault of Number Three, who is the keystone of the arch, so to speak, on which the game rests. If he fails, for instance, his Back will

OUT OF THE GAME.

have two players on to him instead of one, and such a state of things *must* always be Number Three's fault. Numbers Two and One are then likely to get flurried and out of their places as soon as they miss their accustomed support. In the same way if Number Three is a weak point in a team your adversaries will know well that it is good policy to hustle him continuously, as by so doing they will divide your ranks in two and throw so much

The Game.

extra work on the Back as will probably break down his defence.

Therefore from first to last the vigilance, activity and self-control of Number Three must never fail. Anxious about Back, eager to help his forwards, though in return he is buffeted by the enemies' Number Two he must get neither flurried nor weary. For these reasons Number Three should be a judge of pace and able to husband both his own strength and that of his ponies. Of the latter he will need the best he can buy, and even then, unless his stable is a large one, he will find himself riding tired animals towards the end of a match.

Watchful always Number Three should be specially careful about the play in the third period of a fast game, for this is the critical time. He may have had a fairly easy time up to this point and things may have been going well, but it is more than possible that now his forwards, who have been doing wonders against men heavier than themselves, will begin to tire. They will begin to get uncertain and to miss, the ground will seem—and perhaps in reality will be—more bumpy as they grow weary and the game in front becomes sticky. Now is the moment for Three to be on the look-out for chances. Let him whose head has saved his (pony's) heels and who while not shirking has economised his strength, now put forward all his powers and working with

The Game.

redoubled ardour snatch the chances Number Two cannot avail himself of for very weariness. Or at all events if Three cannot attack let him hold the game as it were for a few moments till the forward part of the team regains its power. If Three fails to stand in the gap victory will be checked and the team will waver and demoralisation set in. Or if things are not so bad as that it is always dangerous to let an enemy almost if not quite as good as yourself make a goal at this period of the game. Such a loss may never be recovered and the coveted trophy may pass from your possession for want of judgment, nerve and resolution at one short period of the game. An ideal Number Three—and the best I ever saw was Major, then Captain, Colvin of the 9th Lancers, now unfortunately retired from polo—should be able to make up the deficiencies in judgment as well as in the play of his fellows.

To play Number Three then is desirable almost in proportion to the excellence of your play and your suitability for the post. For though in other positions you may even as Back redeem deficiencies by dash and determination, as Number Three nothing but the soundest and most sustained play will avail you.

A word now as to the ponies. They had better be fast, but they must be stout, able to stay, and above all handy. Neither must they pull. In fact they must be such animals as a man can ride with-

The Game.

out thinking how he is to control them. They will of course fall short of this standard, but the nearer they come to it the more suitable will they be for a really first-class Number Three. How such ponies are to be procured and paid for is another matter and one with which here at least I have nothing to do, though, as I have shown elsewhere, a skilful, patient horseman may do much towards supplying himself with the very best of ponies for the purpose.

A question has been raised as to whether Back or Three is to "hit out" when the ball has been sent behind the goal, and this seems a fitting place to consider it. I should say that if the Three and Back in a team are equally certain players that it is better for Three to do this, but if Back, with whom the decision should lie, prefers to hit out himself, or if he is the stronger hitter of the two, then Three should protect the goal and will therefore be for a time in Back's place. My preference for Number Three as hitter out, other things being equal, is one that I share with Mr. Miller and the late Mr. Moray Brown, and the reason for it is that if the hit-out is successful and Three places his ball well, his team will fall at once into their places and will thus have a better chance of making a successful attack.

The duties of Back in theory are but two, to guard his goal, and to place the ball for his forwards, but in practice they are legion, for in the evolution of the game it has come to pass that Back has also

The Game.

become the leader of his side. The reason of this is not far to seek. The qualities needed for a good Back are rather certainty of hitting—and experience—than extraordinary speed and dash, and consequently the position has come to be given to the older players. This is not of course to say that in a good game Back or anyone else can afford to be slow and

SAVED.

pottering; but that a heavy man, on stout, handy ponies, or one who, though a fine player, is not so fast as he once was, will find ample scope for his talents in this position.

It is of the first importance that the ponies on which Back is mounted should be stout and very handy, for they will have to stand a good deal of

The Game.

hustling, and must be ready to turn sharply whenever their rider sees his chance of putting Number One, or even Number Two as well, off side. The Back must also be able to turn quickly to get to his goal in case of a reverse, and the more speedily he can do so the better and stronger will be his defence. In attack Back should not hang back too much, though this is a not uncommon fault; but he should keep well up to the game, so as to be ready for all chances. His position must however be somewhat regulated by his confidence in the men in front of him. If he can trust them, he may lie further back and devote himself to returning the ball in such a manner as may best suit them: to place the ball, for instance, so that Number Three can pass it on to Number Two, and avoid making the forwards turn by meeting the ball and shouting to them at the same time to go on. To meet the ball, it is true, as I have said before, is a risky game for a weak side; but there are cases in which, with a good team, it is the better play. It is plain that if Back is some way behind, it will be going much more slowly by the time it reaches him, and for a good player therefore there will be hardly more risk in meeting it than in backhanding. If you meet a ball also it is certainly easier to give it the right direction than it is to send it in the desired way from a backhander.

If, on the other hand, Back knows that the men in front of him are not entirely to be trusted, then he

The Game.

should ride more up into the game ready, in those cases which will be obvious enough when they present themselves, to go up and take the ball as he summons Number Three to "Look out, Back," or it may be to turn and take a backhander or race the attacking Number Two for the goal. If the position of affairs calls him to attempt the last, he must turn sharply so as to get a clear lead, for the probability is that Number Two is a lighter man than he is, and is riding a faster pony. A couple of lengths' start goes for much in the short distances that have to be galloped on a polo pony, and Back will generally find that he can get to the ball first, or, even if this be impossible, he can reach the goal before his adversary.

When the ball is nearing the goal, instead of hitting a backhander, Back should use the stroke to his left under his pony's tail, which Mr. Miller advocates under such circumstances. As this fine player points out, a stroke direct to the rear will often fail, because it may strike a pony or may indeed fall into the hands of one of the opposite side, for it must be within the knowledge of all who have watched polo carefully that many a goal has been made by a ball from a backhander being stopped and brought on by the attacking side. The Back should never rest while the ball is in front of his goal, and if he can prevent it going behind the posts in no other way he must hit out behind his

The Game.

own goal. All the chances are in favour of the attacking side which can get and keep the ball near the goal, for luck will often supplement skill, and a pony may kick the ball through the posts or even a nervous stroke from one of your own side may add to the score of your adversaries.

Thus the responsibilities of Back are great both in attack and defence, since in the former he must prevent the ball from getting back and save his side from turning as often as may be, and in defence he must strive his utmost to keep the ball from his own goal. Then Back is also in a position of command, and to him falls the duty of rebuking, exhorting, and rallying his side. Back should, however, be sparing of his tongue; and except he is coaching a young team, he should say no more than is absolutely necessary. To this some Backs may take exception, and may bring against me the example of Mr. John Watson, who, as is well-known, coaches his team constantly. But in the first place we are not all John Watsons, with his exceptional knowledge of the game and his gift of putting heart into his team. One thing, however, may be learned from this player. If Mr. Watson has a weak or nervous man in his team, he does all he can to encourage him and to put heart into him, and if he sees a man really doing his best he will give him more praise than blame, even if not always successful. And with a first-rate team in front he

The Game.

says no more than is necessary. But for ordinary folk to exhort a bad team beyond a certain point is hopeless, and to coach a good one is superfluous. More of course is permitted in this way in a military team than in a civilian, for the Back in a regimental team is, in nine cases out of ten, the man who has made the players in front of him, and the feeling of good fellowship and *esprit de corps* prevent men from misunderstanding or resenting exhortation which with a team of civilians might be the case.

A quality that is absolutely essential to a Back is a steady, dogged pluck and staying power, for he must be able to defend his goal to the last. The moment the defence is broken down the game is lost. For this reason a man is not suitable for Back who is weak physically, or who has a chronic pain in his temper; for in the one case he will not be able to bear the brunt of a resolute attack as he should do, and in the other he will not care to try when put out or discouraged. That Back should have a steady resolution is most important, not merely to the defence of his goal at the moment, but to the future possibility of victory. In a case like the following it may often happen that for half the time of play or more the side which wins ultimately is kept on the defensive.

Suppose the sides A and B—both equally good. A is composed of light, active men on quick ponies,

The Game.

while the average of B is slightly slower and a good deal heavier. For the first half of time A will press hard, but if B's Back is good they will, though apparently having the best of it, shatter themselves and spend their strength against his defence. B, though often pressed hard, will keep together, never relaxing their efforts, though few and ineffectual may be their excursions into the enemies' country, and many the shaves of their goal. Indeed, it is more than probable that A will score once or even oftener ere half-time is called. At this point, however, B's weight will begin to tell, and gradually the lighter side will be borne back from B's goal, and the field of battle will almost imperceptibly be changed to the middle of the ground. There the two sides may circle for a long period of undivided give-and-take play; but to the experienced eye the change in fortune is coming, and there would not be much risk in having a small bet on B. For almost suddenly A will collapse, fairly overborne by the strength of B, and goals will rapidly mount up to the credit of the side against which, in the earlier stages of the struggle, it seemed almost any odds. But such a result would be impossible if B had not a Back who was at once a good player and of a disposition not easily discouraged, for during the time when A was pressing it might easily have been that they made such a score as for the victory of their adversaries to be impossible under any circumstances. Back,

The Game.

however, by his clever and determined defence kept them in check, and thus it is owing to him that his side could make their own strong points as a team felt.

Back is thus a position of great responsibility, but also of immense enjoyment, and most players who have tried the position successfully have shown a great liking for it. It is also an honourable and pleasurable retreat for the old age of the player, or perhaps it would be more accurate to say that it is the reward which awaits the man who has made himself a thorough master, not only of the game in practice, but of its theory and tactics.

It is impossible to close this chapter without some few words on that which is, after all, the central point of the polo of to-day, viz., combination. Without this all other virtues in a team are of no avail. Though mounted on the best of ponies, and having among them the most brilliant hitters, and the most certain players, yet whenever a team which lacks this crowning quality meets another of inferior stamp in many ways, but which is thoroughly well trained and disciplined, the former will oftener than not suffer defeat. Now, good combination being made up of many qualities is difficult to write of, yet no book on polo can be complete without something being said on this most important topic.

What, then, do we mean when we speak of the

The Game.

combination of a team being good? We mean that the players play as one man, and that, like good players at whist they consider their partners as much as themselves. The golden rule of conduct in life sums up the duties of a polo player to his fellows, and the motto "Love your neighbour as yourself" is as binding in the polo field as in the ideal social life—*not more*, remember, or you will fall into the extravagances of self-suppression and will be unable to do your best, or to be of that service to your side which your individual powers ought to enable you to be. A really good player must know his own play and have confidence in himself when it has been proved that he is better than others, and must be able to shout "Leave it" without any misgivings when he sees that he can gain an advantage for his side. Many men fail, on the other hand, in frankly acknowledging to themselves their own weak or inferior points and boldly acting on that knowledge. The good player should know both his strong points and his weak ones, and a first-rate man will be able to appraise others as well as himself justly and impartially and act accordingly. Such a man is of untold advantage to any team for which he plays, for a selfish player, however good in some ways, must always be a weak spot, for he will be thinking of himself, and is sure, whenever the chance arises, to commit the crowning sin of a polo player and shout "Leave it" to another player because he wants

The Game.

the ball for himself. In the result it will matter little if he is impelled to this action by conscious selfishness or from unconscious vanity.

The first step then for the ambitious player who desires to take a good place in a good team is—a certain proficiency in the game and a useful stud of ponies being assumed—to study his own play and that of others, carefully comparing and contrasting the results in his own mind and making the necessary inferences as to the conduct to be adopted when playing with his fellows. Every game to this player will be a match, and he will give as much thought and earnestness to a members' game as if it were the final of the Inter-Regimental or the Champion Cup. I do not of course say that he will get as much excitement and pleasure from it, but I argue that he will not only get more of these than most men, but he will at the same time be preparing himself to take part in first-class matches and to enjoy to the full the delight of first-rate polo, than which there is no more exciting sport to be had save only pig-sticking and hunting at their best.

The suggestions given above show the best way of preparing the individual player to become part of a combination, and it is well known that when men band themselves together for any purpose the force and power of achievement of the collective body is greater than the sum of their individual capacities. If it be not too fanciful to say so, I would suggest

The Game.

that a body of men disciplined and held together by *esprit de corps* create a collective individuality separate and apart from the mere sum of the abilities and courage of the individual men. A regiment, for instance, is a continuous entity, and in spite of retired officers and time-expired men it retains its special character as years pass on. Whatever its component parts, it remains the 10th Hussars, the 9th Lancers, the 13th Hussars or the 17th Lancers, and when we speak of these regiments there is always at the back of our minds a consciousness of the spirit of the collective body which has a continuous history and existence apart from the individuals which at any one time fill up its ranks.

Now polo is essentially a warlike sport, indeed it might almost be called a military exercise, and precisely those virtues which make a good regiment go to the making up of a good polo team. In writing of combination one's mind turns naturally to the polo team of the 13th Hussars, which is the most splendid example we have of the value of combination in the polo field. I shall not, I trust, be misunderstood if I say that they have never had more than two first-class players in their team if we take as our standard of comparison the test of individual brilliancy which is often so misleading. Nor have they been a well-mounted team in comparison to many others. They have as a matter of fact made it a duty not to give extravagant prices for their

The Game.

ponies, and when, in 1894, they won the Inter-Regimental at Hurlingham after a series of the most magnificent struggles, Captain Maclaren openly said that not a pony in their team had cost above £40 in the first instance. Much of course had been added to the ponies' value by careful and thorough training, and this is a fact which in no wise detracts from the lustre of their victories. By means of perfect discipline and combination this team has a record of polo performances which is second to none in the British army, and which has been only rivalled of late years by the Indian polo career of the Durham Light Infantry.

The same reflections apply to the great record in polo established by the brothers Peat in conjunction with Mr. Mildmay and Lord Harrington. In this combination there was one superlatively good man, Mr. Johnnie Peat, but what was of far more importance than individual brilliancy was the perfect trust and confidence that the brothers had in each other's play, while Lord Harrington, as every one knows, is one of the most loyal and thorough players that ever swung a stick.

There was too another point which marked both the celebrated teams of which I have spoken, and this was that they did not chop and change their best ponies. They rode the same animals for many consecutive seasons, for when they had a good pony which suited them, they knew it. Few men indeed

The Game.

will ever reach the top of the tree at polo, and no one, I may safely say, will be consistent in his play if he is always changing ponies. This is a most important point in the coherence of a team, for no man can stay in his place and do what is required of him if he is mounted on a pony that he does not know, or that does not suit him. Still less of course can he do so on a bad pony. The vices of horse-coping and pony racing are the two great enemies of polo, and you will do well to deny the one and avoid the other.

But all this time I have said nothing, it may be urged, as to what combination at polo really is. All the same I have been endeavouring to clear the ground by insisting on those necessary preliminary considerations which will enable each player to take his proper place in a well-organised team. If any player were asked "what is combination?" at polo, he might very truly answer "a place for every man and every man in his place," but yet the definition would be insufficient.

To prove this let us suppose four players to go out to play a match. A will play One, B goes Two, C Three, and D takes Back. Now the chances of the game will soon prove that it is not really possible for the four men to keep always in their own places. It will be found that each man must be thrown out sometimes, and if he only thinks of returning to his place instead of playing the true

CLEARING THE WAY.

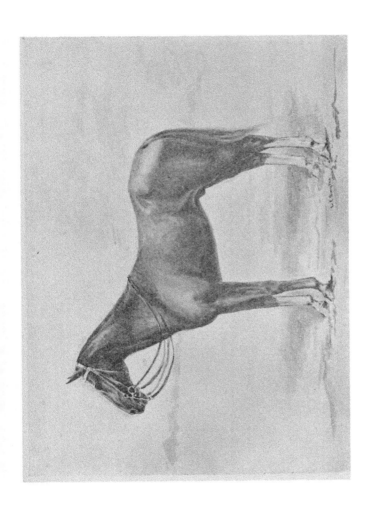

"*JOHNNIE*" (*Arab*).

PLAYED BY MAJOR LE GALLAIS IN THE WINNING TEAM, CHAMPION CUP, 1895.

The Game.

game of combination, and the others in the same way only strive to maintain theirs, it will be seen that there must be continually weak places in the team with the result that the enemy's Back will be going free when he should be pressed, and your own Back at a critical moment may have two players on him. The true idea of combination therefore is not that no man should ever stir out of his place, but that as far as possible there shall always be *a* man in each of the four places.

The leading idea of course is that four players are chosen and arranged in their several positions according to their particular abilities, but in practice every man must be ready to take another's place as occasion offers, remembering to fall back to the original arrangement as soon as possible. There are naturally some inter-changes which are unlikely to take place. Number One, for instance, will not have to go Back or Back come up to One, but on the other hand Number Three may find himself in any place in the game and will often have to act as Back or Number Two. In a good team, then, the men will always be ready to take each other's places, and equally quick to fall back without confusion into their own. That indeed is the first point in good combination, and the next is that each player should support the player in front, giving him every opportunity. The result of this will be that the ball is continually passed from

The Game.

one to the other. Passing may be said to be the supreme test of a team's combination, and when you see the ball placed and passed from one to the other, it says far more for the quality of the play than the most brilliant runs. If therefore in a team each man backs up the other that team will necessarily win many matches.

Let me give an example of good combination. Let A (1), B (2), C (3), D (Back) be playing in the order named. D hits a backhander, placing the ball well at C's right hand. C hits it once, then being hampered by Number Two of the other side hits it forward to B, who is galloping in front. B then gets hold of it and goes on, but after he has hit the ball twice a bump in the ground stops him or he is ridden off. C, who is close behind, and has disengaged himself from his adversary, comes up and takes the ball while B drops back to Number Three. C being again unable to carry on the ball, B once more comes up and races on while A is keeping his front clear. They are not far from the goal, but are being severely hampered, so D, who has been watching and sees that neither B nor C can get a clear shot at the goal shouts "Leave it. Keep them off!" and darts through just as B, with a dexterous twist of the wrist, places the ball for him, and hits the winning stroke. It may be mentioned here that when either Back or Three is hitting the ball, the forwards in front of them

The Game.

should, as far as possible, ride in echelon not directly in front, or the ball may strike either their ponies or themselves, and thus change the whole course of the game.

Now the goal which we have just been considering was clearly achieved by confidence in each other *and*

A SITTING SHOT.

combination, for during the run up while B and C changed places more than once, there was always a Number Two and a Number Three for their side. The worst possible evidence of want of discipline is when a team gets altogether in a heap. This is worse in result than a momentary scattering, though the latter, which is bad enough, may, and indeed often

The Game.

does happen to any team. The players will, however, sort themselves out and show of what stuff they are made by the speed with which they will place themselves ready for play. To see them, however, in a heap shows that their organisation leaves much to be desired.

It will be noted in the instance I have given above that the fancy players carried out the two duties of a polo team, viz., to hit the ball themselves and hinder the enemy from doing so. A team in fact is something like an English political party whose object is to govern the country if possible, but if not, to hinder their opponents from doing so. But with regard to combination of play in a team it may be said to be when four men desire with one will the same object—to make a goal—and take every possible means within the limits permitted by the rules of the game to attain it.

I have said nothing in this chapter on the subject of foul play, because I do not think anything is needed. To all those who have either played or watched polo for some years it will be clear that no game is played with more general fairness and observance of rule. Fouls, of course, occur sometimes, but they are inadvertent and unintentional in nearly all cases. Though, too, there may be occasional differences of opinion on the subject of tactics, yet such are mostly open questions, nor need we prolong this chapter by discussing them.

CHAPTER V.

The Umpire.

The Umpire is comparatively a modern institution and any effectiveness he has dates from a very few years back. At first his sole duty was to canter about the ground while a match was going on, and generally when a question arose he was lighting a cigarette or looking the other way. He then summoned the two Backs and they laid their case before him, with the result that unable to come to a decision he would ride off to the pavilion to reinforce his own hesitation with other people's doubts. For the most part no one thought of referring to him, and indeed the position of umpire was considered as a sort of sinecure for a person whom it was designed to honour, or as a last tie with the game for a superannuated polo player. At the best the umpire was thus like the children of a generation back, expected to be seen and not heard, and he was not supposed to speak until he was spoken to, or to give an opinion unless he was asked.

Since then the umpires have come into much greater prominence, and it is to be desired that their authority should be still further increased. Um

The Umpire.

pires made their first step to a position of authority in India when Lord Roberts took up the question of regulating polo. Players hardly realise how much they owe to the former Commander-in-Chief in India. There had been a succession of serious and fatal accidents on Indian polo grounds. It was said that play was often reckless and dangerous especially

THE CHIEF DANGER OF POLO.

towards the close of a hardly contested match. My own experience, which covers a good deal of ground in India, was that the danger came rather in station games. Little or no supervision was exercised over players and still less over their ponies, and dangerous players and savage ponies were unpleasantly common. The rule about crossing was disregarded, and the practice carried on to a most dangerous extent.

The Umpire.

But the chief danger arose from the number of unbroken ponies that were permitted to play. I myself have been kicked and bitten more often than was pleasant, and indeed I once saw an Indian civilian, now a judge, dragged bodily from the saddle by the slack of his riding cords by a pony which was in pursuit. Yet the biter and kicker were small evils compared with the badly trained, underbred, hard-mouthed, yawing brutes that were far too common on the field. Most of the fatal accidents I have known were caused by these animals getting out of hand and charging some other player, with the result that one or both were brought to the ground.

Thus polo came to be in bad odour with the military authorities, and its total suppression was openly talked of and threatened. There were colonels and others who thought that it was a good opportunity to put down a game which they considered endangered the lives and the efficiency of their best officers. For as a rule the best officers were keen polo players then as now. The players themselves were not altogether wise, no doubt. They had come to care more about the speed of their polo ponies than the goodness of their chargers. It was a trouble to a smart cavalry colonel to see that his officers would spend as little as possible on their chargers and a good deal more on their polo ponies. There was therefore considerable pressure put on Lord

The Umpire.

Roberts to suppress the game, or to do what came to the same thing, to put down the annual tournaments. The Chief, however, was himself a sportsman and a fine and enthusiastic horseman, and he saw the advantages of polo and determined to regulate the game—to mend it and not to end it. The plan he adopted was to direct the formation of an Indian Polo Association, and sketching out the lines of the reforms which would satisfy him, he left the details and the way of carrying them out to a representative body of players. The result was satisfactory, and from the discussions of the I.P.A. the modern umpire emerged a much more responsible and important official than before. He was no longer to wait to be asked, he was responsible for checking all foul and dangerous play, and was empowered to stop the game at any time, or to order a dangerous player or pony from the ground. At the same time the hustling rule was added, and the umpire was charged to see it observed. Thus the umpire in India was endowed with responsibility and some pains were taken in his choice. It was not till later that his position in England was improved, and he was given the power of intervening in the game at his discretion. Even now, however, umpires are not made sufficiently responsible, nor is enough care exercised in their choice.

One reason for this is because a good umpire is by no means easy to get, for the good qualities that

The Umpire.

are required of him are many. In the first place he must know the rules well, and this is by no means so common an accomplishment as might be supposed. Nothing is more usual than to find a man very ignorant of the rules of a game at which he constantly plays, and the umpire must do more than merely get a knowledge of the laws which govern the play. He must have studied them carefully and considered beforehand what his decision should be on doubtful points. To this end he should think out some of the more likely cases of infringement that will probably arise, and try to find out what are the opinions on doubtful points of the best players. Then he must have played the game so that he can readily place himself in imagination in the position of the players. No man can possibly make a good umpire who has not played and watched good polo carefully for some time. Then last but not least he must be able to make up his mind quickly, and having done so must uphold his decision quietly but firmly. When a man is placed in a position in which a decision of doubtful points is likely to be asked of him, he should of course do his best to come to a right decision, bearing in mind that he *must* decide something, and that it is better even to come to a wrong decision than to none at all.

It is I think an open question what the best position for an umpire is. Mr. E. D. Miller in his book advises that the two umpires should divide

The Umpire.

the field between them and each confine his attention to the part of the ground which is, so to speak, under his control. Another and perhaps a better position for an umpire is alongside (not of course too close to) the Back of the team opposing the one for which he is umpiring. My reason for thinking this is because Back is or should be in a position to command his team, and so see what is going on in front, and also because it is between Back and One that the most disputes arise. It is important to Back to put One off side, and it is equally important to One not to be put off side. The question is often one of inches and the umpire must be near enough to see exactly what happens. It follows that the umpire should be well mounted on a handy pony, for he must remember that while he should not be too far away to see what goes on nothing can excuse his being in the way of the players at a critical moment of the game.

But when I have given this list of requirements, I have not by any means exhausted the qualities demanded of our ideal umpire. Great tact is required to know when to intervene. *De minimis non curat lex* is a good maxim for an umpire to remember. That is he should not let any extreme conscientiousness lead him to intervene unless the intervention is necessary either to stop an injustice to a team or to prevent danger to a player.

"Don't fuss," "Don't worry," are good pieces of

The Umpire.

advice for the umpire. Another important matter is that he should be as impartial as he can. It is a very common thing for umpires to become partisans, and this is difficult to prevent. All soldiers know that umpires at manœuvres often become ardently partisan and excited on behalf of the side for which they are umpiring, and from judges they become advocates. This failing must be carefully avoided, and as a rule, since there is much human nature in mankind, men should not umpire when their own regimental or club team is playing. The more detachment of mind an umpire can preserve the better.

There is certainly one point in which umpires are needed to interfere more than they do. The danger of Indian polo is in falls on the hard ground, but the peril in England is from the stick. Players ought to be much more careful than they are, for all the serious accidents of late years have taken place from blows from the stick. In cases of wild play a word of caution from an umpire would be useful, since players in the heat of a most exciting game often forget rather than disobey the rules. The future of polo largely depends on the discretion and power of the umpires. As the game develops the presence of an efficient umpire will become more and more necessary, and on his shoulders will rest the responsibility of preserving players from accidents that arise from a careless or wilful breach of rules. It is not too much to say that the umpire

The Umpire.

is chiefly to blame for accidents, if through want of care and attention he has neglected to give the warning required or even to stop the game. To say that he "did not see" is, or should be, no excuse. He is there expressly to see what goes on. But although from the above a great deal may seem to be expected of umpires, yet nevertheless it is not really an unpleasant office. As umpire you see a game in a way no one else can do. You get a pleasant ride, and you are, if an enthusiast about polo, continually learning more of the game. On the whole it is probable that the more is required of umpires the better qualified will be the men who will be willing to act. To be an ornamental dummy is only attractive in inverse proportion to the abilities of the man of whom action is demanded. To occupy a position respected for its authority and influence, and to become a power has its attractions in small things as well as great. To be an M.F.H., for instance, is not always a bed of roses, but men are willing to spend largely to occupy that position, because it is of the nature of an opportunity for the use of powers of command, and so it will be with umpires. Besides, let players in their prime to-day consider what a pleasant tie to the game this will be for them as they grow older. There may be men who would rather umpire the final of a hard fought Inter-Regimental tournament than play in a duffer's game.

CHAPTER VI.

MANAGEMENT OF THE POLO CLUB.

THERE is no kind of association for purposes of sport that is easier to manage than the polo club. The reason of this is not far to seek. Polo players are as a rule a very friendly set of people, and tolerant, as the members of a club should be, of each other's smaller failings. Yet even a polo club is not without its difficulties. One of the greatest of these which confronts every manager is to get good players to put up with novices and indifferent performers in members' games.

Polo is a game which has grown slowly into popular favour, and in its early days, when players were not too numerous, the keen beginner was always sure of a welcome to make up a side. But as the number of players increased, the necessity of keeping a strict roster became evident to polo managers, for thus only could each member of a club be sure of his game. The authorities naturally strove to give every man a chance of showing what was in him by putting him into a match in turn with others as far as possible his equals. Then the early leaders of the game in this country, and Lord Harrington in particular, spent much time and took

Management of the

infinite pains in the encouragement of novices and in teaching them how to play. There is indeed probably no game or sport in which the course of the beginner has been made as a rule more smooth. It is true of course that of absolute duffers there are fewer that try their hand at polo than at any other game of strength or skill, for a man must have some real liking and aptitude for the game to make the necessary outlay and master the preliminary difficulties of hitting a ball off a galloping pony over a more or less rough surface. Yet is it hardly too much to say that there is no game in which a man can be of real service to his side with so little actual skill. Obedience, loyalty to his side, a readiness to give way to better players, and the by no means universal capacity of making ponies gallop, are all that are necessary to make a player tolerable in an ordinary game or even in a match of second-class players. It is probable that such a player will be actually preferable to the brilliant, uncertain, and selfish man who never rides an adversary quite off, and who looks upon the polo ground as an exhibition field for solitary runs, and who is always on the look-out for chances of gallery play. No beginner who is really keen is made to feel himself out of place in a polo club, and by the presence of the novice on the field, members learn to give and take in a way that is almost unknown in other games.

"SHY LASS" (First Prize Polo Pony Brood Mare, Hurlingham, 1896).
THE PROPERTY OF MR. NORRIS MIDWOOD.

Polo Club.

Let me now take the various needs of a polo club in order and see at what we should aim.

The Ground.—This I put first, inasmuch as it is the first need of a club, and every effort should be made to secure a full-sized one. The increased pace of the play in the present day and the size of the ponies now used point to an increase in the size of the ground in the near future rather than to a diminution. The proper size, according to rule, is 300 by 200 yards, and the ideal ground is as level as possible, and should be laid with soft and springy turf of "immemorial antiquity." Yet there should be a natural slope sufficient to drain off the rain water and prevent any part of the ground becoming boggy and slippery. It will, however, be found more often than not that the ground is not level or the turf as good as could be wished, and then it will be necessary to set to work on such improvements as the time and means at your disposal will allow.

The expenditure necessary for relaying an unsatisfactory field with good turf is considerable, but when the means are available it will undoubtedly be found more economical in the end to do the whole business thoroughly and at once. For this purpose old turf must be bought and carefully laid by an experienced man after the ground has been levelled. This was the plan adopted by the Hurlingham and Ranelagh Clubs when they made their new grounds, and it has been very successful.

Management of the

The majority of clubs, however, will not perhaps be able to find so large a sum as is requisite—the Hurlingham ground must have cost at least £3,000—and then they must do what they can. Much, of course, can be achieved by carefully improving the turf that is in existence by cutting and rolling and by judicious top-dressing. The greatest care in manuring the soil should be taken, and I would warn managers against ordinary stable manure as being worse than useless. Better than anything else, in my opinion, is bone dust with sifted garden earth spread over the top. Mr. E. D. Miller in his book (p. 70) recommends the use of peat moss, and on some soils this may answer, but from my own experience I should say is never very good. A plan sometimes adopted is to sow grass seed in spring and autumn, but this again is not of much use. Clover, too, should be avoided altogether, and I say this with authority, for I believe that I am responsible for the sowing of some clover seed on the Ranelagh big ground, and the grass so produced has been found very slippery and treacherous. If the grass should be weak and unequal, the best and cheapest plan in the end—always supposing the best of all is out of your reach—will be to cut out the poor and worn patches and lay down some good sound healthy turf, fencing it round and giving time for it to heal up the divisions between itself and the old grass.

Polo Club.

In this process sheep will be found useful, but only if they are penned, for they will not do much good if they are allowed to wander at will over the ground. A good plan is to pen them on one quarter of the ground and shift the pens till they have been all over the field. It is perhaps needless to say that the sheep should be removed during the polo season. Early in the spring the grass should be rolled thoroughly, and as soon as possible in dry weather or when the sun is hot, a mowing machine with the boxes off be passed over it. The cut grass left on the field will keep the moisture in the ground and is in itself an excellent top-dressing. If there is good rain followed by a fairly fine spring, the turfs will have knit together well before the opening of the regular polo season in May, but if the season should be late, it may be necessary to put off the opening of the ground for a fortnight or three weeks. But it must be remembered the time for polo is so short in England that any curtailment which can be avoided is undesirable. Polo managers and secretaries, I may remark in passing, will do well to recollect that the object of a ground is to be played on, and, therefore, to be too tender of it is to defeat the end for which it was made.

When at length a winter's care and thought aided by a favourable season have given to the anxious Manager a parallelogram of brilliant emerald grass, smooth and flat, and the pleased members praise the

Management of the

ground and think the end is achieved for which they have been so anxious, then in truth the work has only just begun. To make a good ground, indeed, is much, but to keep it in order when made is much more, and the latter will need the utmost diligence and oversight on the part of the manager. There is no need to be nervous about playing on the ground, for a well kept field will stand five days a week in ordinary seasons. One day off is needed for cutting and rolling, and the other rest day can be Sunday, so that on every other day the ground can be used without fear of injury, provided, of course, the weather is not exceptionally wet. The possibility of playing after rain will naturally depend somewhat on the nature of the soil. For instance, the Hurlingham ground wants a rest after heavy rain, while that at Ranelagh is better to play in wet than dry weather, as it has a soil that will not stand watering. In the Phœnix Park NINE ACRES play is possible when the spectators are standing in puddles two inches deep, as those will recollect who were present when the great match for the A.I.P.C. was played between the Freebooters and the 13th Hussars.

The amount of play which a ground will stand therefore depends on several things, the soil, the season, and the quality of the turf, but on none so much as on the treading in of the ground after play is over. This is a most important point. Directly the last game is over, from twelve to twenty men

Polo Club.

should be formed in line under the guidance of a responsible person, and marched up the ground. Every wound made in the turf by stick or hoof should be noted, and the missing piece of turf put back in its place by hand if necessary, and then gently and firmly pressed in with the foot. This work cannot be attended to too thoroughly or carefully, for the better it is done the more play the ground will stand, and it is, I need hardly say, a work that, unless carefully looked after, is not unlikely to be scamped. But, if well done, the reward is certain, for after a hard day, when the ground has been cut and scored till it looks more like a ploughed field than a polo ground, the following afternoon may see a broad flat green expanse smiling a serene invitation to you to gallop over its velvety surface. Those who have seen the ground at Hurlingham during the week of the Inter-Regimental Tournament will know what can be done in this way by efficient labour and careful superintendence.

The ground being of the greatest importance is naturally the manager's first care, but after having laid out his ground and got the surface as level as may be, he has still to consider the question of boarding. There was for a long time a difference of opinion as to the use of boards. The late Mr. Moray Brown was strongly of opinion that the board was no advantage to the game. But the logic of facts is against this view, and boards are now quite established in favour, nor can any polo ground be considered complete without them. The game with boards and without is naturally somewhat different, and players are accustomed now to calculate on the effect of the boards on the course of the ball. The boards should be nine inches high and painted a deep red, and they should have a very gentle slope made up to them on the inside of the ground. Great care must be taken not to get too long or steep a slope or the ball will go out almost as if there were no boards. A very easy slope is enough to bring the ball down and to prevent it from lying up. The slope required is just and only just sufficient to keep the ball from hanging under the boards.

The Pavilion is also a necessary adjunct of the polo ground, but its convenience is very much a matter of the funds in hand. The best pavilion is, of course, the one at Hurlingham, but that cost at least £2,000. The neatest for a country club is one like that at the Stansted Polo Club near Bishop Stortford. For comfort and convenience, combined with a small cost and a tasteful appearance, it would be difficult to beat this little pavilion. There is one point which, while it necessarily adds to the cost also adds greatly to the convenience of spectators, and that is a roof from which to view the polo. To see a game properly one must be above the players, and I know no better position in point of height and

Polo Club.

relation to the view of the players than the middle of the pavilion roof at Hurlingham. To describe a game as Mr. Moray Brown used to do, it is almost necessary to be above the players. Moreover, I find that matches are much more difficult to describe at Ranelagh, where the pavilion is not well placed to give a bird's eye view of the ground. You never see the game there as a whole, and in consequence can only describe isolated instances of skill. The way to write a good description of a game of polo is to try to see the whole match and to have photographed on your mind the positions of the teams at the critical points of the game. You cannot, of course, really put a whole match on paper. I well remember the late Mr. Moray Brown asking me to go to Ireland to provide him with descriptions of the All Ireland polo team and the Inter-Regimental. The notes were transcribed and written out, and the reply came back, "Very good, but you are too copious; if I had printed your notes as they stood, they would have filled eighteen columns of twelve hundred words each." Then I began to understand that a description of a polo match did not differ from higher classes of literature in that the art lay in knowing what to leave out.

But this is a digression. To realise the true nature of the game it is necessary to look down upon the players, and for this purpose, at least, the roof of a pavilion is necessary. For the rest, a pavilion should have hot and cold water laid on and a fair number of baths and dressing rooms, or if there is a club house, these are better in the house, as at Ranelagh, than in the pavilion. Refreshments should also be served at a convenient bar, and tea, if ladies are admitted, should be served in all parts of the building. Again, I must note that the waiting arrangements in the pavilion at Ranelagh are worthy of imitation. Although not always perfect, they have shared in the steady improvement which has taken place in the service of this well-managed and charming club.

Stables.—Clubs round London will find it desirable to provide stabling for members' ponies. It is possible to do this at a reasonable charge to members and yet to make a moderate profit for the club. There are two ways in which the stables can be managed; one is to farm out the arrangements to a responsible man, who pays a fixed sum per stall to the club and makes what he can. This is the Hurlingham plan. Or the club can keep the stabling in its own hands, appointing a resident stud groom who will be responsible to the secretary and committee. This is done at Ranelagh and has worked well. At this club £1 1$s.$ per week for each pony without a groom is charged, or 18$s.$ 6$d.$ if the owner sends a man with him. The cost of building the stables was not high, the eleven stalls to the right of the stable-gates costing something

Polo Club.

under £150. The smallness of the cost, it is true, was owing to the pains taken by Mr. Dare, the head gardener, but it could be done nearly as cheaply anywhere with care. In this case no contract was made, but the bricklayers and carpenters were paid by the day. Very elaborate stabling is not required, since the ponies will only be in them for about three months. How much the provision of stabling is appreciated can be seen from the fact that long before the season is begun, every stall and bin is engaged at Ranelagh and late comers are obliged to go outside. Mr. Tom Jones's well-known polo stables at the "Red Lion" supply a good many polo ponies with a temporary home where they are well cared for. I believe the wants of polo players in the matter of stable accommodation are being catered for elsewhere in the neighbourhood of Putney.

The Secretary and Polo Manager.—This is a most important person in every polo club, and to his enthusiasm and management the polo club will owe its success, perhaps its very existence.

The Rugby, Stansted, Cirencester, and Eden Park Clubs are almost the creation of their Hon. Secretaries, while every one knows what polo at Hurlingham and Ranelagh owes to the managers there. To describe the qualities required by a polo manager would demand a chapter by itself, and then we should be no nearer endowing any particu-

Management of the

lar manager with them. But there are two gifts he must have—tact and a knowledge of the game. The secretary must be continually watching the play of members so that he may be able to make up good and even sides in members' games. The members' game, be it remembered, is the backbone of the club, and the better and the more even these are, the more likely the club is to be able to put a good team in the field for the county cup or any important tournament. By carefully watching members on the ground, the polo manager will learn the play of each man and will find out whether he is of more use as forward or back. There are certain useful rules which polo managers and secretaries will do well to bear in mind. The first is that if two teams are tolerably even in play the heavier will win, and that in working out sides of fairly good players weight must be considered as well as skill. After watching with unusual care a very large number of matches both in India and in this country, I am convinced that weight tells very much at polo, and that when the sides are otherwise equal the betting would be in favour of the heavier team.

Another point to be noticed is the staying power of a player. This is partly a matter of training and partly of constitution. This you can observe best in that third period which is generally the turning point of the game when play has been level.

Polo Club.

There are a certain number of players who are brilliant for ten minutes, and who after that are of no use at all. Yet another point worth noting is that ponies are of more value than men unless the discrepancy between the latter is very great.

CAPTAIN WALTER SMYTHE.

If there were (to put an extreme case), two teams, one quite first-class, and one good second, and the second were much better mounted, it would be not unlikely that they would score over their opponents. Of course it must be understood that the excellence of ponies referred to, is not merely that of shape

Management of the

and make, but of being thoroughly good at the game. Or we might put the matter thus. A first class man + a moderate pony = second class man + a first-class pony.

It is the duty of a polo manager to arrange a succession of matches in such a way that while the club is represented on great occasions by its first team yet there shall be matches of such a quality, that as many men shall take part in them as possible. It is impossible to have a really good succession of players unless you give your beginners a chance of showing what they are made of. The play of men in matches is often astonishingly good, while on the other hand there are good players in members' games who invariably disappoint you in a match. This last kind of player is the man who cannot really play in a fast game or will not ride off. An excellent and a most interesting form of competition is the handicap tournament. One should always be held at the beginning of each season. It is useful to enable one to see what sort of form the different players are in, and it also helps players to get into their game quickly. The usual method of arranging a game is for each man to put his name down and then for the secretary or polo manager to settle the players in teams. The teams are then drawn against one another and the tournament played off. Another plan is to put all the names together and draw the teams, and then

Polo Club.

handicap them by making the scratch teams start a certain number of goals on the minus side The latter is not a very good plan as there is so great an element of chance and luck in polo that you can only handicap a man roughly. Any more rigid system would not be successful. Another difficulty of handicapping is that you cannot tell what pony a man is going to ride, and this will necessarily modify his play a good deal.

Of the scale of subscriptions to the club I have said nothing because these must vary with the necessary expenses. A polo club, however, is not in itself an expensive thing to keep up, and a very moderate subscription should keep the ground and pavilion in a state of efficiency. In country clubs there is always a small revenue available from honorary members who, in return for a guinea or two a year, receive tickets for the reserved enclosure and pavilion for the matches, or gymkhana sports, which always make a good and popular finish to the season.

CHAPTER VII.

Polo in India.

THE main principles of polo are of course everywhere the same, and the previous chapter on the game would in nearly every particular apply to players wherever they might be. In India, however, there are some important differences, both in the rules of play and in the circumstances of the game. The following hints are intended more for the help and guidance of intending visitors to India, who are drawn thither, whether on duty or pleasure, than for those who make a longer stay in the country. To the soldier going out for the first time, this chapter will possibly be of some interest, but it is chiefly intended for the benefit of the civilian (in this term including all officials who are not soldiers) or the globe trotter.

Such advice is in fact little wanted by the soldier, for he will at once find himself one of a community who will, if he have the luck to be gazetted to a polo-loving regiment, probably teach him to play, and put him in the way of getting all that he requires. All classes of intending polo players will, however, be glad of some hints as to what they shall take with them. The best outfit, remember, is the

Polo in India.

smallest, and when I went out I regretted the purchase of more than half the things I took with me. But, nevertheless, there are certain articles of equipment for man and horse that should be taken. To speak of the man first: There are two articles of clothing difficult to get satisfactorily in India —breeches and boots. These, therefore, should be taken, and it will be as well to carry with you all you may have of either,—new or old.

Then I should advise you to take spurs and bridles. It is difficult to get the latter to suit you in India; not that there are not plenty, and by good makers, to be had, but the bits are as a rule too long in the cheek, and the snaffles are too thin. The headstall and reins you can get without difficulty, but they do not take up much room, and it looks neater to have your reins stitched on the bits.

As for saddles, take what you have, for a good English saddle is always useful, and is at any time worth money. You will not lose by taking out saddles, but you must go to a saddler who has made something of a specialty of providing for Indian horses and ponies. There are certain makers, such as F. V. Nicholls, of Berkeley Street, who found favour in the eyes of Indian horsemen, and whose handiwork will always meet with a ready sale. To these I should add a few good English stable brushes, as well as some spare girths and stirrup-leathers. A good general rule for an Indian outfit

Polo in India.

is that everything—except a tall hat—which is useful at home is useful out there. Those articles which are necessary by reason of the climate can be procured quite as well, and a great deal more cheaply, when you reach the country.

When you arrive in India the first thing to be done is to buy some ponies. If you are joining a regiment that plays polo, this will present few difficulties. There is generally the opportunity of taking over the best of the ponies of someone retiring or going on leave, or probably there will be a regimental club (polo) which will mount you. In any case, the way will be made easy for you under those circumstances. A man who is willing and able to play polo, or is ready to learn, is sure of a welcome and an excellent training in his regiment, and to this we may leave him, for there is none better. To the civilian or to the would-be soldier player who joins a regiment which does not play, the case presents more difficulties. There are certain counsels, however, which can be given without hesitation. One is, do not buy ponies in the station where you are unless you are quite sure you know all about them. The demand for good polo ponies is great, the supply very limited, and regiments that play seldom or never allow a good pony to go. Then be sure you avoid advertisements. Remember the words of the man who said he never knew how good his horses were till he saw them

Polo in India.

advertised for sale. Never under any circumstances buy a pony without seeing it yourself, I might add except when you can get a thoroughly trustworthy friend to see and try it for you; but perhaps that is a possibility hardly worth considering. But advertisements, remember, are as misleading as they are specious. Many years ago in India I bought in haste (and repented at leisure) four ponies from an advertisement. I had been ordered to a distant station where polo was regularly played, but where it was well known ponies were hard to buy. When my four newly-purchased arrived none of them were worth anything as polo ponies, and only one was a tolerable animal of any sort. The price paid for any one of the lot was more than the four were worth together. From a somewhat varied experience I should say that unless your opportunities are extraordinary and your purse deep, do not in India attempt to buy made ponies. Moreover, never under any circumstances buy from or sell to a friend.

From the foregoing, the conclusion, then, has been arrived at that in India the polo player should buy his ponies in the rough, and train them himself. This will be found an interesting business, and there are three ways in which it may be done: First, you can buy Arab ponies in Bombay when you land, and take them up-country with you, which is perhaps, on the whole, the best plan; but you must

Polo in India.

make up your mind that each polo pony you get in this way will cost you from Rs.800 to Rs.1,000. Suppose, for instance, you buy four, and pay Rs.400 a-piece in the first instance, which is a very moderate price for a good pony—and you may easily give double—your four ponies by the time they are landed at any up-country station will certainly cost you another Rs.200 each, bringing the price up to Rs.600. Of the four the probability is that only two will make good polo ponies, and the others will be sold for say Rs.200 each, leaving you with two polo ponies at Rs.800 a-piece, at the lowest computation. I do not say that so you will have done badly. On the contrary; for if the two stand work, and improve, they will give you a great deal of pleasure, and will be worth anything up to Rs.1,800 when you wish to sell. To buy Arabs as the raw material means, then, a considerable outlay, as compared with the means at the disposal of most Anglo-Indians, when they start life in the East. If, however, a man happens to have the money, then to buy the very best you can is good economy. But economy is among the luxuries denied to the poor. Thrift the needy may have, but not economy.

So much, then, for the first plan. The next is to buy from a native dealer some country-bred ponies; and if you adopt this plan, avoid sweeping generalisations. All Indian dealers are not cheats any more

Polo in India.

than all English and Irish dealers are. Because most men, honourable in other matters, have a somewhat lax morality in respect of horses, it is not wise to assume that respectable dealers of any hue—who have, remember, a reputation to keep up—will allow themselves the same laxity. One rule applies to buying horses or ponies all the world over, and that is—above all things do not be too clever.

The best dealer in country-bred ponies in India is Aslam Khan of Lahore. If you go to him and tell him what you want, and treat him as a gentleman —which in his own country he is—you will most likely get a good pony from him. Remember that when a country-bred is good, it is very good, though really first-rate ones are rare. Ponies can also be picked up at the fairs. Some years ago Batêsar used to be a great place for ponies, and a few were bought every year at Amritsar. The horse and pony fair in India is one of the most interesting sights in the world to a lover of horseflesh. There are collected together horses and ponies in some thousands, and in every colour, shape, and size. The screams of the horses and ponies, the shouts of the natives (who always speak at the top of their voices), the galloping hither and thither of animals that are being shown off to purchasers, the heat, the dust, the mixture of colours, all make up a most exciting scene. The would-be purchaser needs all his coolness to buy at such a gathering ; but prizes are to

Polo in India.

be secured by those who have wit, courage, and coolness for the business.

Having by one of these methods once got together your train of polo ponies you must proceed to get them in hand. The method of training suggested in a former chapter will be found as useful in India as it is here. One of the great faults of Indian polo is that the ponies are often not half broken. Some such dialogue as the following may often be overheard in the polo ground : " Hullo, Smith, that's a nice looking pony ! " " Yes, bought him to-day from Hussein Khan the delâl (broker)." " Will he play ? " " Don't know ; I am going to try him now," and off the speaker goes straight into the game. No words can be too strong to condemn such action. An unbroken pony is a danger to his rider and to every one else on the field. I do not hesitate to say that station games in India are often spoilt because the players have unbroken ponies. Such animals when ridden on a curb are a blunder, when ridden in a snaffle they are a crime.

I have found that in practice the ponies which take most readily to the game at first are not those which make the best ponies in the end. Eastern ponies are often nervous and require gentle handling, and those that seemed shy at first often make the best players, after a careful education. The reason, of course, is that in India the ground is hard, and the game, if it is at all a good

POLO IN INDIA.

Polo in India.

one, is pretty fast, for second-class polo in India is certainly faster than a game of the same sort in England. The new pony, perchance, plays well; and so pleased are you with your purchase, that instead of giving him about three minutes you ride him for a full ten minutes or more. The pony has probably had one or two blows with stick or ball, a few digs with the spurs, and has been twisted about and galloped in a way that makes both mouth and legs sore before he comes out of the game. Now the most marked characteristic of a horse's intellect, scanty enough in other respects, is his memory. Consequently, next time the pony will decline to play, and will be voted useless, whereas with time, patience, and gentleness he has in him the making of a good pony enough.

If you have played polo in England you will not find much difference in the rules when you take up the stick in India. The process of assimilation between the English and Indian rules has been going on for some time. The last instance of this is that the Indian Polo Association has adopted the Hurlingham rule for off side in place of their own rule, while, on the other hand, Hurlingham has adopted from India the rule as to "riding off," and some of the penalties for fouls. But it will be the better plan to note some of the leading differences in the rules. In the first place, the ponies are smaller in India than England. The height of the

Polo in India.

Indian polo pony was fixed at 13·3, under the impression—a mistaken one in the opinion of many players—that a small pony is safer than a big one. What really matters is the training and schooling of the ponies, not their size. Then the bamboo root ball is larger than the English willow root, the latter having a diameter of 3 inches, as against 4 inches of the former. When a match is played the time allowed is less. No match in India must exceed forty minutes, which is now divided into eight periods of five minutes each. Ponies can be changed at the close of each five minutes, but by a recent ruling the game will not be stopped for players who wish to change ponies during the five minutes. Those who ride off the ground do so at their own risk. The newcomer from home will also be struck by the size of the Indian polo ground, as full-sized grounds are rare in England. The Ranelagh Club, it is true, has lately made one, Cirencester has two, and the New Eden Park Club at Beckenham one, but nearly all other grounds in England are short of their full length. Then the newcomer will notice that in India there are no boards. As a matter of fact, these were introduced by a happy inspiration at Hurlingham as a correction of the small size and irregular shape of the match ground there. They were found to be so great an improvement to the game that from that time no ground in England has been considered complete without them. They are not, so

"*RANGOON*" (*Burmese Pony*).

THE PROPERTY OF MR. KINDERSLEY.

Polo in India.

far as I know, used anywhere in India, expense and the white ant forbidding.

In the Indian rules it will be found that the duties and powers of umpires are laid down with care, and, generally speaking, the player will find that the power of the umpire is more of a reality there than in England. In addition to the umpires, are two goal referees, officials whose duty it is to stand near the goals to decide disputed points, as to the scoring of goals, and the passing of the ball over the back line. Then the player will find that there is a penalty for hitting behind his own back line to save a goal. If this is done it is then open to the opposite side, at their discretion, to hit off from the nearest corner, all the defenders being ranged behind the back line, and the attacking side being thirty yards away from the goal line. This is no doubt right, and there ought to be a penalty for hitting behind.* There is another excellent rule in India which directs that "no player shall at any time place his own stick over, across, or under the body of an adversary's pony" (Rule 31 I.P.A. Laws of Polo). I am glad to see that this rule has been added to the Hurlingham code.

Then there is another institution which we shall never see here, and which it may be hoped will some day be removed from the Indian book. This is the

* This penalty is now imposed by the Hurlingham Rule 14, as revised.

Polo in India.

subsidiary goal, which was introduced in deference to the idea of the authorities that playing off ties was dangerous. Consequently each side scores subsidiaries, one point for each time that the ball crosses the back line within eleven feet of the goal posts on either side. An example of the evil of this was shown, when, in 1877, the Durham Light Infantry beat the 16th Lancers for the Inter-Regimental tournament at Meerut, by one subsidiary, a conclusion which was unsatisfactory to both sides, for a subsidiary may or may not be a fluke. The chances are even either way.

A question which is often asked is, " Which is the better game, the Indian or the English ? " I should say that the play at the best English matches was better than play in the Indian tournaments, the size and pace of the English ponies and the difficulties of the ground calling forth the very highest efforts of skill in the player. On the other hand, station polo is distinctly higher as a display of average polo than members' games. More men play in India, so the choice is larger in forming the sides, and as players have fewer distractions than at home, they practise more.

The best individual player I ever saw was in India, and that was Heera Singh, late of the 12th Bengal Cavalry, afterwards of Patiala. On the other hand, the best team I ever saw was in England. But there is a fact which shows how

Polo in India.

vain such comparisons are. With a few very important exceptions, our best English players have been trained in India, while a good English team, like that of the 4th Hussars, showed itself able to hold its own directly after landing at Bombay, and to win an important tournament. India, on the whole, is the best school for polo players as for war, and for the same reason—because in that country is to be found more opportunity for practice than at home.

CHAPTER VIII.

POLO IN THE COLONIES AND ABROAD.

ENGLAND and India undoubtedly stand first in the polo world, and next to them comes America, North and South. It is however from South America that the players come who have adopted the English game. The Argentine colonists and natives have taken ardently to polo, and have achieved great success therein. The methods of the Argentine players in England in 1896 were not different in any respect from those of the English, except that they had not attained the same perfect combination that may be seen in a first-class English team. This is true of all Colonial players, who are fine horsemen and well mounted, but who play a more independent game than we do now in England. But greater combination is only a question of time, for the players are all most enthusiastic about the game, which is exactly suited to countries where horses are cheap and time is precious, and where men can only spare a comparatively short time for exercise. Polo everywhere is the townsman's athletic sport, and it is in the neighbourhood of Buenos Ayres, Sydney, Melbourne, and Brisbane, that the most flourishing of polo clubs exist. In New Zealand,

Colonies and Abroad.

polo is becoming very popular, and from the photographs which have reached me, I should say that they have splendid material in ponies to work upon. Most of these clubs follow Hurlingham rules, but generally they use smaller ponies than is the custom in England. In South Africa, too, polo has taken root, but so far as I can gather, the late troubles have prevented its development. I hear, also, that there is some scarcity of suitable ponies, but that can only be a temporary want. Directly the game becomes known it is sure to make its way, and I cannot help thinking that the exhibition of first-class polo, which the South Africans have had during the stay of the 9th Lancers, will give a decided stimulus to the game. In North America, the popularity of polo is undoubted, and with characteristic originality, our cousins have worked out a code of rules for themselves. The principal differences between their rules and ours are as follows :

1. Ponies are 14·1 hands in height.

2. Provision is made for matches between two and three a side, as well as the standard teams of four.

3. Goal referees, or judges, are provided for as in the Indian rules.

4. There is an excellent rule which forbids players to appear without their club colours on, and another which inflicts a fine for being late.

5. A ball hit out behind by one of the defending side in order to save a goal counts as one-fourth of a goal, and, I presume, though it is not laid down, that in the event of a tie would turn the balance.

6. Every man is handicapped with the number of goals which he is considered worth to his side. If two teams play together, the side which has the largest number of goals in the handicap has to allow that number to the other side.

Thus :—

    A. B. C. D. play E. F. G. H.

Suppose they are handicapped thus :—

    A. 1   C. 2   E. 2   G. 1
    B. 3   D. 4   F. 4   H. 5

Then E. F. G. H. team start with two goals to their credit, which have to be wiped off by the other team before they can be on level terms.

The effect of these rules appears to me to give more weight to the individual player than with us. Combination becomes of less importance than individual brilliancy, and from what I have heard and read of American play—for I am writing from hearsay only—I should think this was the case. It will also be noted that there are no penalties for fouls except that the game is stopped and the ball thrown in. The American players I have seen have had great dash and pluck, but on the whole

Colonies and Abroad.

I should think their game was less scientific, though not less exciting than ours. It is impossible without a personal acquaintance with American play to say whether the result of their code will be to differentiate the transatlantic game from ours in any important particulars or to set up an American school of polo players. One thing is certain, and this is that the Americans have taken to polo very warmly and that they have for it an enthusiasm not less than that which is shown over here.

Of foreign polo there is not much to write as polo on the Continent is simply a flourishing off-shoot from England. But already there are some fine players among the French and Spanish teams, and the names of Escandon, Le Jeune, and De Madre will occur to every polo player. The pluck and keenness with which the players above-named, and several others, have taken to the game we all know, and I think everybody would be glad to see a French or Spanish team successful in a tournament over here. We all recollect the memorable game played on the Ranelagh ground between the French and Spanish teams in 1895. Polo, which is the nineteenth century representative of the joust, can hardly fail to commend itself to men of two races so renowned for chivalry as the French and Spanish. In addition to these clubs I have heard of one at St. Petersburg that is in process of formation.

Polo in the Colonies and Abroad.

What others there may be I know not, but the world-wide spread of the game which had no code of rules till the original edition of the Hurlingham Rules was put forward in 1875, is remarkable enough, and may reassure those who fear that the game will not retain its hold on the affections of men.

Two sports widely different indeed in all else, polo and bicycling, are alike in this—that they have come to stay. Of the other places where polo is played there is no need to write, for in Malta, Gibraltar, Cyprus, Jamaica, Samoa, and the rest, it is only English polo on foreign service, like the soldiers who are its best supporters.

CHAPTER IX.

Polo Ponies.

To write on polo ponies is a difficult matter, for I do not feel that I can add a great deal to what Mr. Miller has written on the subject of the different breeds. In the main I agree with all that this writer has said in *Modern Polo*. Each breed of ponies has its merits and its defects, and when we are considering what we shall buy we shall find our choice limited both by what we can get and what we can afford. The man who means to play in first-class matches will find that in practice he is now limited to English or Irish ponies. No others have the pace, the power, and the courage required to carry a man of average weight through the periods of a fast tournament game. The above sentence looks somewhat sweeping, but on reflection I am unable to modify it except perhaps by saying that possibly Australian or New Zealand ponies might hold their own if we could get them, but so far no considerable importations of either has taken place. Practically in England we are confined to two classes of ponies, the English and the Eastern, and under these two main heads I shall proceed to consider them.

Polo Ponies.

English Ponies.—I do not know that I need describe the ideal polo pony, for such word painting is only calculated to excite false hopes. Moreover, for most people it is useless, since we pick out a polo pony for precisely the same points for which we should choose a hunter. Naturally we buy the best we can get. Two things are absolutely necessary for the beginner at polo, and are really far more important than any theoretical questions of make and shape. The first is that the pony must know the game. The second that the man who buys him should be able to ride him. If you really mean to play polo you must get a pony that can teach you, for you cannot be pupil and master at the same time. Moreover, if you can afford it, you will always find it better and in the end more economical to buy ponies with established reputations, even though they might not win prizes at a show or come up to our ideal of a miniature weight carrying blood hunter. If you have money and not leisure you *must* buy made ponies; if you have leisure and little money you *may* succeed in making one really good polo pony out of every five promising ones you buy, and I think you will be lucky if you average that. One thing is certain, that both for pocket and pleasure it is better to have few and good ponies rather than many and moderate ones. It is wiser if your means are limited to buy two first-rate ponies than four moderate ones, and it is

Polo Ponies.

also more economical, for the good ponies will be worth their price at any time if you take reasonable care of them, and you will save the keep of two indifferent ones. It is never worth while to keep a bad pony in your stable, and by this I do not mean a pony that is a little slow, or that is a bit of a cripple, or a delicate feeder, but one that pulls, shies off the ball, has a pain in its temper, will not hustle, and cuts it at a pinch. Becky Sharpe observed that it was easy to be good on £5,000 a year, and with the command of money and patience there is no doubt you will be able to get together ponies good enough to satisfy you. What about judgment? Well, if you buy ponies of reputation you will naturally have bought the result of someone else's judgment. But however good the pony, he is no use remember if *you* cannot ride him, and before taking him over you must absolutely have a trial in the game, which will, as a matter of fact, always be granted if you ask it. It does not follow that because one of our great players performs well on a pony that everyone else can do the same. Perhaps, however, you are not so ambitious. You do not wish to play polo in first-class company, but simply to hold your own in members' games. To you polo is the most delightful and exciting of pastimes, the best means whereby in a busy life you can get exercise, health, and the forgetfulness of worries. In that case read the next

Polo Ponies.

section on Eastern ponies, for it is among these that you will find what you want. To return, however, for the present to home-bred ponies, the supply of these is much less than the demand, though they are to be obtained in the rough by men with eyes to see and patience to train them. The best have hitherto come from Ireland, for the reason that in that country men love blood better than action, and you will find fewer steppers and more galloping ponies in proportion there than here.

The demand which arose some few years ago for harness ponies and hacks coupled with the influence of the show ring caused a very great infusion of hackney blood. A great many of the good-looking ponies driven in Ralli cars were crosses of hackneys and Welsh mares. These were for harness good enough, but for polo—useless. The bicycle has now displaced the harness pony to a very great extent, with the result that I think more ponies suitable for polo and riding are being bred in England than formerly. There are, however, certain districts in England where good blood ponies can be picked up, for example, in the Essex Hunt country, the Badminton and the V.W.H., countries which have all yielded some good ponies of late years, though none of them have as yet had time to make names for themselves at polo. Mr. Townsend, the Secretary of the very flourishing Cirencester Polo Club, tells me that the supply of ponies in that district is good,

Polo Ponies.

and many people will remember the smart lot shown by Mr. F. Gouldsmith at the Polo Pony Stud Book Society's Show at Hurlingham in 1896.

Unfortunately little is known about the origin of some of our best English ponies, but one thing is plain enough, that they are as nearly thoroughbred as possible. Two of the best-looking ponies of the lighter bloodlike stamp which have been brought out recently, viz., "Little Fairy" and "Sorceress," are well bred enough to win the Derby. To the man with leisure, patience, and horsemanship looking out for such ponies, training them will be an interesting occupation. He will be well carried and on the whole at a reasonable price. Let him, however, have no thought of profit. He may make polo ponies but he will not as a rule make money. Some few men indeed may have done so, may still be doing so, but they are the exceptions which prove the rule. There are one or two things that are useful to bear in mind in buying the raw material to train. First avoid all suspicion of hackney blood. I should regard a pony with distrust that bends his knee much in the trot. Avoid, too, a sour looking head or a sunken eye. Reject a pony too long in the back or with doubtful hocks, remembering, however, Mr. Miller's true words that sickle hocks are no disadvantage to a polo pony. Personally I would never buy a pony that had not a good rein. Of all paces the walk is the one to test a young raw pony

Polo Ponies.

by. If you take a pony a mile or so down the road and then put the reins on his neck, and let him walk towards home you will know a good deal about him by the time you get off his back. If a pony walks away at a good pace and with a good swing, if he does not trip or stumble, if he is a *good* walker you may safely buy him. No rule about horseflesh that I know is absolutely universal, but in buying a pony if you look after his walk you may safely leave the gallop to take care of itself, provided always he is a fairly well-made, well-bred animal, and as I said before, has not too high action in his trot. No man who tries a pony from a country dealer or off a farm can learn everything about him. By the walking test you can learn more than in any other way. Another useful maxim is always be ready to buy and equally ready to sell. When you see a likely pony buy if you can, you never know but you may be buying the one supremely good animal which comes to every man once in a life-time. On the other hand, directly you are pretty sure that a pony is no good send him to the nearest auction and let him go. It is far cheaper in the end than keeping him to fetch the price you put him at. Nothing is dearer than coping though. I will acknowledge it has an evil attraction, but it seldom brings money, and it generally costs us friends. To sell a bad pony (by auction without reserve) is cheaper than to keep him, and may, if you choose your time of year wisely, in

Polo Ponies.

some cases turn out better than you have a right to expect.

Eastern Ponies.—Under this head I may group together all those ponies which reach us from India, Egypt, Syria, or that are known as Barbs. The latter may be taken first, as of the least consequence. There are very few good Barbs playing now, and there always will be, because the Barb is not as a rule a good pony, and is not much imported. If you hear of a Barb with a reputation being in the market, and he is not too expensive, he may be worth buying, but I have no great partiality for them, as the American said of pickled herrings, "I kin do with 'em, but I don't hanker," and this I think expresses the real opinion of many good judges concerning the Barb. Lord Harrington's "Awfully Jolly"—being a useful polo pony, was and is a very successful sire—will be brought up against me, but I shelter myself under an agreement with Mr. Miller's opinion that "equally good results would be obtained by a cross with a high caste Arab." Might we not say better, since the Arab is a finer breed than the Barb?

Of the other Eastern ponies we may say that they are good in proportion as they approach the standard of the high caste Arab, but that individual ponies of very various types have made good polo ponies. In this country we have, as a matter of fact, to judge the Eastern pony rather at what

Polo Ponies.

he is than what he looks, and very few come over here from Egypt or elsewhere. There can be no doubt that the importations of Arab blood has been valuable for breeding purposes. There is no better pony for the members' game and second class match than the Arab. There is no need to despise him because he cannot, as a rule—and there are exceptions in all matters of horseflesh, as I have already pointed out—live with the best English ponies. Many players will not often require great speed, and will get more fun out of good Arabs than inferior Irish or English ponies. The Arab is handy, sound and easy to play as a rule, but does not like deep ground, and is a bad hack, nor is he fit for a very heavy man. For a moderate player, however, of fair weight, riding not over thirteen stone, there is no better polo pony. One advantage of the Arab is that he improves very much as a rule with time and good keep, and as he matures late the buyer will often find out that he has a much better pony than he thought.

Of pure Arabs but very few reach this country at all. The best specimens of the high caste Arab that have come to England in recent times are those imported by Mr. Wilfred Blunt. Those that come from India are bought from inferior tribes which breed expressly for the Bombay market, and are not nearly so careful about pedigree as the Arabs. No doubt a certain number of well

Polo Ponies.

bred Arabs do reach India, but they are comparatively few, and come more by chance than anything. I have seen some Arabs having every appearance of belonging to a high caste among the ship loads which the British India steamers bring down from the Persian Gulf. Amid the heavy, rather coarse animals which are generally to be seen among "gulf" Arabs, it is easy to note the superior quality of those descended from a better strain.

There was a bay Arab which used to run in Galloway races (14 hands) in Sind, which was the property of Sir Henry Mand, and had every appearance of being a well-bred animal. This pony was the winner of many races. In the same way I have seen some beautifully bred Arabs among so-called Egyptians. But whatever his breeding and wherever he is found, the Arab has the same virtues and the same faults. He is sound, hardy, and of a good constitution, but he does not go well, as a rule, on soft ground, as he likes to hear his feet rattle. He is not, of course, so fast as an English pony. As a rule, however, he is an easy pony to play, learns the game readily, and with careful training is a bold and rather clever hustler. The best taught ponies in this way I have ever seen are those belonging to the Jodhpur polo team, and they are carefully and systematically taught to jostle. The clever way in which these ponies

Polo Ponies.

will evade one heavier than themselves and will shoulder another off in a close struggle for the ball is worth seeing.

The Arab is an intelligent animal, and his courage generally prevents him from becoming shifty as he gets older, though to this, as to all other rules, there are most undoubted exceptions. Arabs are, as a rule, good ponies for a beginner, and are always useful to save better animals in members' games, but they are not and never can be in the first rank as polo ponies in England.

Of other Easterns, the Indian country-bred is undoubtedly the best, and I have seen some very good ones indeed. But a really good Indian country-bred is very rare, and many, therefore, are never likely to come to this country. Even in India, to get a really good one is not easy. The largest dealer in Indian ponies, which have a large infusion of Arab and English blood, is Aslam Khan, of Lahore in the Punjab. Many a pleasant morning have I spent in his yard trying his ponies and riding the promising ones out of a new batch one after another. But though there were many to choose from—and Aslam is both a good judge and a good horseman—there were comparatively few really good ones among them, and those easily fetched prices that would make it unlikely it would ever pay to bring them to this country. Yet I suppose most Indian polo players, in looking back on their experience,

Polo Ponies.

would say that perhaps their pleasantest mount had been an Indian country-bred.

Australasian Ponies.—These again are very good, but so far very few have come to this country. The pictures of " Chance It " and " Nimble" show to my mind that they are breeding a very high-class polo pony in Australia and New Zealand. With the opportunities which they have for horse breeding, and the great extension of the game in that country, more attention will probably be paid to breeding ponies than has hitherto been the case. If our Australian fellow subjects do take it up, they will be sure to produce something good. On the other hand, the length of the voyage and the consequent risk and expense of freighting ponies over here will prevent the Antipodean breeder from becoming, as he otherwise might be, a serious rival to our home producer in the market for ponies in England.

American.—The North American ponies can reach us more easily, and those that have been seen in this country are fairly good. Mr. T. B. Drybrough has taken great interest in them, and has imported some good ones from Montana; but it seems to me that to compete with the English and Easterns, which at present hold the field, any foreign pony must be either much better or much cheaper than the former, and this cannot be said of any Americans I have seen. The most that can be said is that the best are as good as English ponies

Polo Ponies.

of the same class, and if they can be imported and sold at a profit at from £40 to £50 a-piece they would find a market, but it is much to be doubted whether this can be done.

Argentine Ponies.—From what I have seen and heard the Argentine ponies are the most likely to win a place for themselves in our English market. It is true that we have never seen a first-rate Argentine in this country, but those that have come over are so stout, so handy, and seem to take to the game so well that given size, pace, and quality, there is no reason why they should not make an important part of the polo pony supply of the future. Horseflesh is cheap in Argentina, and it is probable that good, well-bred ponies could be raised there and exported to England at a very remunerative price. It is said, however, that well-bred ponies in South America are rather apt to be bad-tempered, but this defect, probably, is not so much constitutional or hereditary, as the result of bad handling and breaking in their early years. The Argentine method of breaking a pony is, to say the least, hard, and though it may do for cattle ponies or for those destined for rough work, yet, as a polo pony's temper is one of his chief virtues, it will not do for him. There are few people out of England who have better polo than the Argentine men. The teams we have seen over here have taught us that. And while they have played on

Polo Ponies.

our grounds they have also taken notes till they have learned most of what we have to teach as to the class of pony best suited for a high-class game.

South African Ponies.—Polo is yet in its infancy in South Africa, but when politics become more settled and prosperity returns the game will no doubt increase in popularity. It is indeed so essentially the game for the busy man, that it is likely our fellow-countrymen who are more or less engaged in commerce will take it up warmly. Whenever this time comes there should be no lack of ponies, for pony-racing is already a favourite sport in the country, and the demand for good and fast ponies is therefore considerable. The South African pony is remarkably well-bred, as he has at least three or four strains of blood; that he is merely stunted by his treatment, the following extract from an excellent article in *Country Life* (Vol. i, No. 3) will show:

" To the English reader a thoroughbred horse of 14 hands seems an anomaly, perhaps, but the degeneration in size is in no way attributable to the breed, but is due to the fact that they are stunted in their growth from the foal period upwards. Take as an example the *modus operandi* of one of the most successful pony breeders in Natal. This gentleman's mares and fillies, from the time they are foaled until they ultimately furnish a meal for the ubiquitous vulture, roam at large in a 5,000

Polo Ponies.

acre paddock, untouched and for months often unseen. The foals are dropped in the spring, about October, and continue to thrive until March or April, when the winter commences to set in, and the grass is nipped off by the severe frosts and the biting cold winds that blow off the snow-covered Drakensberg Mountains. How the poor creatures contrive to subsist through the hard winters, on the scant herbage they manage to pick up, and without shelter of any kind, is a mystery. However, a large proportion do get through until the following spring, which they meet in such an emaciated condition, that it takes them at least two or three months' grazing on the new grass to recover from the effects of the severe ordeal of starvation, wet and cold, through which they have passed.

"This leaves them, practically speaking, some four months only in the year in which to grow out; and consequently they seldom attain a greater height than 14 hands at five years old, when they are full grown, and before which age they are of not much use for galloping purposes.

"The particular troop to which we allude averages some 200 of various ages, and most of them are the descendants of some twenty fine handsome mares, cast and sold from the ranks of the 17th Lancers at the conclusion of the Zulu War in 1879.

"The stallions run with the troop in the spring, but are taken up and stabled throughout the winter.

Polo Ponies.

'Glastonbury,' who won the Northumberland Plate in the 70's; 'Beauclerc Boy,' a son of 'Beauclerc' of Middle Park Plate fame; 'L'Agulhas,' by 'Buckstone'; 'Hesperus,' by 'Morning Star' and 'Chevalier'—the last three being Cape-bred horses and thoroughbred—have severally reigned as Sultans in this harem.

"The colt foals, which are castrated as yearlings, are for sale at four years, the average prices ranging from fifteen to twenty guineas. The buyer rides into the troop, makes his selection, and the youngster is cut off from the rest, driven with some old horses into a kraal or paddock, where, with the aid of a long bamboo pole and a running noose of brayed oxhide or reim, as it is called, he is lassoed round the neck and choked down at the purchaser's risk. Accidents rarely occur from this 'choking down' process, and it has the advantage that a youngster so treated is never known to develop in after life the vice of reining or pulling back, when tied up in the stable or hitched up by the bridle."

The pony thus bred is wiry, active, hardy, up to great weight, is not too expensive, and is, in fact, in every point except one, an ideal pony. So far as I have been able to gather he is not very good-looking, but after all that is a minor point especially as he has the very best of legs and feet.

Polo had scarcely taken root in Johannesburg when the late troubles upset all arrangements, and

Polo Ponies.

turned the minds of sportsmen to other and more serious matters than those of sport. So far there are comparatively few polo clubs except where there are English soldiers. The advent of the 9th Lancers, one of our best polo regiments, is likely to show the dwellers in that part of the world what good polo really is. Then with the demand for ponies the supply is ready to follow, and South African polo ponies should take a place which at present they can hardly be said to do.

It will be seen from the facts noted above that so far the market in England is confined to English and Arab ponies, and therefore in this country it is practically not much use to consider other breeds as breeds. Single ponies or small lots coming into the market must be taken on their merits and may be considered by buyers with reference to their own capabilities, needs and pockets. The pony should be bought to suit the player and the class of game in which he will find himself, but it may be taken as a general rule that a good English pony in any class is better than any other if you can get him. If an English pony is not procurable at a suitable price then Arabs are the next best.

CHAPTER X.

THE STABLE MANAGEMENT AND WINTERING OF POLO PONIES.

THIS is not a subject on which I can hope to write much that is new. Yet though good advice has often been given on this point, a good deal of bad management undoubtedly prevails. As a matter of fact even the best grooms have strong prejudices, and it very often happens that polo ponies are entrusted to careless or inexperienced lads who, if they do not absolutely neglect their charges, yet certainly are very injudicious in the care they bestow on them. If an owner has not the time to look after his stables himself he ought, at all events, to see that there is an intelligent and capable man at the head of affairs. It may be taken for granted that condition is of the same importance in the polo as in the hunting stable. The routine of all stables is alike, and I need not, therefore, go over familiar ground. There are, however, certain principles which we may lay down and certain faults which we must, if possible, avoid in our management of polo ponies. It is a truism to say that condition is of the utmost importance. The pony that is short

The Stable Management and

of work will be full of tricks for the first three or four minutes of play, and will hang uncomfortably on the hand during the latter part of the time. A polo pony's work is of an intermittent character. He is asked to exert himself to the utmost of his powers, for from an hour to an hour and a-half or two hours during each week, and as his work during this time is akin to that of the race-horse his condition should be similar. To attain this is no easy matter when we consider that in the case of the race-horse trainers, who are necessarily men of unusual powers and observation, spend a lifetime in learning how to bring horses out in such condition that they may do their very best during the short space of time when so much is asked of them. The analogy between the polo pony and the race-horse must not, of course, be pushed too far, but it may be taken for granted that the general principles in the management of each are the same. One of the first efforts of a trainer is to learn the peculiarities of every horse under his care, and though polo ponies are generally treated pretty much as if they were all alike, yet they vary as much as race horses in their constitutions and dispositions. They therefore need the same amount of study. One important point is to find out how much food a pony can eat with advantage to himself. This is a matter in which horses and ponies vary a good deal, but an experience of racing ponies

Wintering of Polo Ponies.

in India leads me to believe that it is possible by careful observation to find out exactly what quantity of food a pony can assimilate with improvement to his condition. As a general rule it may be taken for granted that polo ponies are overfed. Grooms have many failings, but the man who steals food away from his horse is very rare indeed. He does not, however, like trouble, and he is apt to lump down the pony's corn before him without much consideration as to the quantity he gives. Nor does he pay always the attention he ought, to see that the manger is cleaned up. Three full feeds a day is enough for any pony as a rule, and the variation will be generally in the direction of requiring less. The polo pony should have very little hay that has not gone through the chaff-cutter, but a little green food on off days helps to keep the stomach in order. On Sundays a pony will be all the better if he has little or no corn, and instead three bran and linseed mashes, the latter being boiled to the consistency of a jelly. Ponies so treated will be found to come out on a Monday morning fresher and brighter for this diet, for the digestive organs are better for a rest as well as the legs.

And though ponies get too much to eat they generally get too little to drink, or perhaps it would be more accurate to say that their water is given to them at the wrong time. One of the things

The Stable Management and

even the best grooms dislike doing, and this often from a sincere conviction that it is bad for the pony, is to leave water in the stall. Yet it should always be done, for I firmly believe there is no one thing which tends more to keep a pony in health and condition than this. You will find, however, that there is nothing which it requires more resolution on the part of the master to effect. Every time the pony coughs or is a bit out of sorts the man will gently hint that its cause is "swilling all that there nasty cold water." Not liking it himself he can scarcely realise that it is good for his charge.

There is another point which is of great importance, and that is that there should be a good supply of fresh air in the stable, and that the temperature should not in any case be higher than that of the atmosphere outside. If the weather is chilly put on a rug, but never, night or day, should the stable be without a plentiful flow of air through it. Far be it from me to advocate draughts, though I sincerely believe that a draught is far less dangerous than stuffiness or a hot-house atmosphere.

Another most important matter to be attended to is grooming. A pony should have plenty of rubbing, as much indeed as your groom can be induced give him, but *no washing*. It is a very common practice to wash polo ponies all over. I have seen it done on the polo field, and when at the Ranelagh Club have observed grooms wash-

"*THE BEY*" (*Arab*).

FORMERLY THE PROPERTY OF CAPTAIN GORDON MACKENZIE, R.A.

Wintering of Polo Ponies.

ing their ponies industriously, but it is a most objectionable practice and should be strictly forbidden. It would not matter so much if the pony was always thoroughly dried after his ablutions, but this is too often not the case. The washing in cold water checks the flow of perspiration, and a pony that is constantly washed will never have the bright, healthy gloss which we see in those animals that are honestly groomed. Only the dock, sheath and feet (not legs) of a polo pony should be ever touched with water.

Exercise long, slow, and regular on off days is also most necessary to condition, and in this matter also polo ponies come badly off. A pony should walk and trot at least the equivalent of ten miles a day, and this is a duty a good deal shirked by grooms, as we all know well. If a large stable establishment is not kept the master should help by riding one or more of the ponies out hacking, or if there be some soft ground available a little practice with stick and ball will be good both for the pony and his master. Polo ponies should be exercised with a large smooth snaffle, or better still, an india-rubber bit. If it is necessary to put on a double bridle, great care should be taken to sew up the curb chains in leather—good hands are as rare a gift for the groom to possess as for the master.

It does not seem needful to enter into a long dissertation on the subject of saddles and bridles,

The Stable Management and

because the rules that apply to polo ponies apply equally to all other horses.

With regard to saddles, a perfect fit is more absolutely indispensable at polo than on other occasions. A good many ponies are spoilt by being hurt by the saddle. Moreover, it is obvious that an imperfectly fitted saddle requires to be girthed more tightly than one which is exactly suited to the pony's back, and there is no doubt that tight girthing is not only a source of discomfort to the pony, but a frequent cause of vice and ill-temper. Next to the fitting of the saddle, its size is a matter of importance.

Many polo saddles are too small, whereas it is impossible to have one too roomy. It does not look quite so smart, it is true, but it improves the average horseman's play, and is much easier for the pony. As to bridles, nine ponies out of ten will go in a light double bridle, but of this I have already written in the chapter on "Pulling Ponies." Nor do I propose to speak of the case of sick ponies. The less physic there is in the stable the better. In most cases where a veterinary surgeon is not required, a few days' rest, and a few bran and linseed mashes will do all that is needful. It may be borne in mind that most equine ills have their origin in want of care, and it is no bad plan if ponies are ailing and off their feed, to change the groom, or at all events to look far more carefully into your stable

Wintering of Polo Ponies.

management yourself. Bad or careless feeding, or stinted water, are at the root of most stable evils. Of course in this category are not to be included the cuts, wounds and bruises which are incident to polo. On the principle that prevention is better than cure, every pony should have a pair of polo boots fitted to him, and these he should wear, and no others, every time he plays. If you cannot trust your groom, there is nothing better than the Rugby Club polo boots, which are recommended by Mr. E. D. Miller. These can be got at Mr. Clarke's, of Rugby. But if you have a good man, then I should prefer bandages, provided they are properly put on. When a pony comes in from a hard game of polo, the groom should put on a flannel bandage dipped in water as hot as the hand can bear it. Over this a dry flannel bandage should be placed and left on for two hours, when they may both be removed, and a dry bandage substituted. Ponies should be exercised, and should stand in bandages, but these should always be removed at night when the groom takes his last look round. For open cuts or wounds a mixture of Iodi-form and vaseline is a sovereign and rapid remedy. Polo ponies should be carefully watched for any sign of lameness. A little care and rest will often stop the setting up of an inflammation which may develop into a more serious matter.

Care, observation and method are necessary in

The Stable Management and

the stable, and if the master cannot give them himself it will be advisable for him to find a trustworthy man who will take a pride and pleasure in the care of his ponies.

When the season is over and polo players are scattered in all directions, when shooting and hunting claim the attention of those who for some three or four months have been devoted to stick and ball, the question arises as to what shall be done with the ponies. If you have good ones the worst thing you can do with them is to sell them. Prices are at their lowest in the autumn. It is wise nevertheless to take advantage of the autumn sales to part with those for which you do not care. A pony that does not suit you is not worth his or her keep for the winter unless indeed you have a suitable farm on which to turn them out. And this is no doubt the best way to deal with polo ponies in the winter. To turn them out in a situation not too exposed and where they have shelter at will is a capital plan. Polo ponies turned out should have at least one good feed of corn a day, and the quantity should be increased in February before they are taken up. The good ones will then come up fit and strong, and the indifferent ones if got into condition will naturally fetch better prices at the spring sales, and in the meantime will have cost very little indeed. This method of wintering is the best and cheapest, provided that the ponies are in a

Wintering of Polo Ponies.

place where the owner or some trustworthy person can cast an eye over them from time to time. It is the plan for the best and worst of your stud. The intermediate ones should have a rest and then be made to earn their corn as covert hacks, light weight hunters, or between the shafts. This plan, though not without its drawbacks, is much better than an idle existence in boxes, on peatmoss, or sawdust. A year or two ago I had a number of good ponies under observation that were wintered in boxes at the Ranelagh Club. The circumstances were advantageous: we had a good stud groom and the ponies had every attention, yet I came to the conclusion that it was not a plan to be recommended. I should prefer either to turn the ponies out, to work them, or even to sell them outright at the close of the season sooner than try it. Ponies so wintered cost more than animals turned out to grass. Idleness breeds tricks, they get no exercise to speak of, they eat a good deal, and lay up a store of inside fat so that it is half way through the season before animals so wintered are fit to go. Now a polo pony should be ready to do his best by May 1st, or even sooner, if he is wanted for the opening of the season at Rugby. Ponies wintered in boxes practically require to be taken up and put in work about the middle of January, just at the time when the ground is often like iron with hard frosts or drying winds. But the pony that has had

Stable Management, etc.

steady light work, or that has wintered at grass, takes a very much less time to get fit. In fact he is soon ready for the beginning of the season when games are not fast, and after three weeks' work for an old pony, or five for a young one, he will be in the pink of condition.

CHAPTER XI.

Pulling Ponies.

OF all the faults which a polo pony can have, pulling is undoubtedly the worst, for even supposing that his rider can hold him, the pony that pulls will destroy the game of the average player and take something from the excellence of the best. The perfect pony should require no more pressure on the rein than is necessary to stop and to turn him at the right moment, or to get him into exactly the right position to enable his rider to hit the ball to the best advantage. Of course, some men will say that if you do not pull at your pony he will not pull at you. But this is a warning which it is not easy to observe in the excitement of a game of polo, and to many very fair riders it may be said to be impossible. Yet it must not be forgotten that the pulling which is so fatal to the game is as often the fault of the rider's hands or want of nerve as to some defect in the pony itself.

This chapter will only deal with those pullers which are made and not born. For the animal that pulls in all hands, and which cannot be steadied by even the best of riders, is useless for the game and should be forbidden as dangerous. By far the worst

Pulling Ponies.

form of puller is the keen nervous pony which simply goes mad with excitement and has a temperament which in a human being we should describe as hysterical. That sort is incurable. Then there is the pig-headed and stupid puller which may indeed be ridden, but is hardly worth the trouble, as

PULLING IS UNDOUBTEDLY THE WORST.

nothing worth doing can ever be effected with him. And lastly, there is the kind with which only we are concerned at present, the pony which pulls because he has been or is badly ridden. Of this class of pony some will pull always if once taught to do so, while others will only try it on with riders they do not like or who do not know how to manage them.

Pulling Ponies.

For, as is well-known, ponies that do not pull an ounce with one man will catch hold resolutely with another. The celebrated "Dynamite," for instance, which Mr. "Johnnie" Peat used to ride with a loose rein, pulled hard when he first had her, and it was a whole year before she could be brought into a game at all.

So again "Gold," which I agree with Mr. Miller in thinking one of the best weight-carrying ponies now playing, is inclined to catch hold sometimes; and I could mention half-a-dozen other well-known names of ponies which would pull in all but the most skilful hands.

Sometimes, for example, a pony which is nothing particular as a player in one man's hands will turn out well in those of another, even though both men be first-class riders. An example of this may be found in the case of "Skittles," which was certainly not regarded as in the front rank of ponies while Mr. Peat had her, but which, since Captain Daly bought her, has been among the most brilliant of modern polo ponies. Something, too, depends on the kind of game in which the rider plays. The pony which would go kindly in a galloping game with first-class players, would soon learn to pull in a slow, sticky game. That is, in fact, often the way ponies first learn to pull. A man who is a beginner buys a pony with a high character from a first-rate player, and forthwith proceeds to play in members'

Pulling Ponies.

games with others no more skilled than himself. The ball is missed over and over again; it sticks among the ponies' legs, or has to be raked out from the boards, and the pony is galloped two strides, then turned, and twisted, and stopped. In such a game even a fair horseman will sometimes find himself unsteady; and although he would probably indignantly repudiate the assertion, the chances are that he will steady himself almost unconsciously by his pony's mouth. This the pony will undoubtedly resent, and the consequence will be that he will begin to fret and then to pull. On each succeeding day his owner will find him harder to turn and more difficult to steady, and it will be fortunate if, after having learned that the immediate neighbourhood of the ball results in casual blows with the stick or jogs on his mouth, he does not take to shying off the ball. If a pony is a determined and resolute puller—and there are some that can hardly help being so from their conformation of neck—there is no room, it is true, for him on the polo ground; but it is well always to remember that there are scores of animals that pull because they are too good for the game they play in, or for the man who rides them. Now, however good a pony is, he is of no use if he pulls. There are but two players with whom I am acquainted who can ride ponies that ordinary men would call pullers with apparent comfort and satisfaction: The one is Sir

TURN YOUR PONIES.

Pulling Ponies.

Humphrey de Trafford, who may be seen playing Back in the steadiest manner on a pony which would take most men into the next county before they could stop it; the other is Mr. A. Rawlinson, whose ponies do not pull, so far as I can see, because, as he always rides them as fast as they can go, *ils n'avaient pas de quoi*, as the cherubs said when they were asked why they did not sit down.

The whole secret of not having pulling ponies lies, in fact, in yourself, and the way you learn to play polo. The first thing for a beginner is to have ponies that are absolutely easy to ride. This is helpful if you are a good horseman, and necessary if you are an indifferent one; nor does it matter much whether the pony is handsome or ugly, fast or slow. There are two golden rules, on the observance of which depends the player's future in the game: One is, always to ride your pony as hard as you can in any game you play—(you must do your slow work in solitary practice);—and the other is never during your first two or three seasons to use any pony you cannot ride easily at practice in a snaffle, or at most an indiarubber bit, and in a game in the plainest and simplest of double bridles. If you observe the first of these rules you will find that you will gradually acquire the art of hitting at full speed, which cannot be mastered except in the game itself; and, moreover, when you step into the first class among polo men, and play in matches against a fast

Pulling Ponies.

and accurate team like that of the Freebooters, you will be able to ride the fast thoroughbred ponies you will then require without making them pull by rolling about in your saddle, or fretting them with untimely tugs at the mouth.

There is one other cause, however, that may make ponies pull, and that is, briefly, want of condition. The majority of polo ponies are high-couraged animals, and are highly fed; and even the best of them will catch hold when they are fresh, and hang on your hand when they are blown. Every polo player must have noticed how much pleasanter and easier his ponies often are to play during the second ten minutes than during the first, the reason of course being that they were wildly fresh for the first five minutes, and rather blown for the last three of the first period of play. In the second period, the edge having been taken off them, they economise their strength, play no vagaries, and apply themselves to the task of pursuing the ball, which they understand to be the object of the game as well as you do. The great danger in playing a pony above itself is, that it is much easier for an animal to learn to pull than it is for you to cure him, and therefore "the short way with pullers" is, never to let them begin. Polo ponies want good and steady work, and plenty of it; and if you happen to be a good-tempered man and patient, there is no person whose company will be so profitable

Pulling Ponies.

to them as that of the master. If a new pony or an old favourite shows signs of pulling, as ponies will sometimes, take him at once for a hack. Ride him in the park in the morning, if in London, or if you are at Aldershot or the Curragh take him about with you whenever you can. Leave him standing outside shops and offices, ride him in traffic, and if you have a light boy that can ride, let him come with you on another pony, and change from one pony to another. There is nothing like steady and persistent hacking for keeping a horse's back down, and making him quiet and handy.

Lastly, there is the standing martingale, which is a most important element in training a pony for polo. Every one who has seen the best native teams playing in India will understand how much of their success is due to their ponies being so perfectly manageable and handy. The secret of this lies in the native method of using a bridle. A native of India does not hold on by the bridle, and therefore he prefers a sharp bit which will stop and turn a pony quickly, but which he will use not at all except for such purposes as bridles were intended for. Yet, inasmuch as ponies pull because of the varieties of their tempers and the faults in their shape, the native polo player has recourse to a standing martingale. Against a standing martingale affixed to a nose-band a pony can pull as much as he will, which is not very much,

Pulling Ponies.

without hurting himself, tiring his rider, or deadening his mouth. The native plan, then, is to find out in practice what length of martingale each pony requires. This is ascertained by the simple method of taking it in or letting it out till it is seen just at

THE STANDING MARTINGALE.

what point the pony ceases to pull. It is astonishing to notice how tightly some ponies heads are tied down, though in practice it seems to interfere very little with their action. English and Irish ponies are, for the most part, much better shaped about the neck and have better shoulders than Indian ponies,

Pulling Ponies.

so that they would require no great amount of tying up. But if the Indian plan is followed—and it seldom fails—a single rein on the bit will be the best bridle, bearing in mind that it is never to be used except to stop or turn, and that the rider must rather fall off—or if no one be looking, grip the saddle to steady himself—than hang on the pony's mouth. If, indeed, he does the last, he will very likely come down. If the player be not too proud, a breast plate is a capital thing to steady himself by. This will be found a most effectual cure for both pulling ponies and heavy hands. Very few people are aware how much they depend on their bridles till they try to do without them. How few of us could emulate the celebrated feat of Captain Trotter, who, when Master of the Meath, lost his bridle and rode through the rest of a fast run without one, guiding his horse by the hunting crop in his right hand? In teaching the art of riding there is, in my opinion, far too little attention paid to this. The pupil naturally holds on the bridle whenever he loses his balance. How prone we are to steady ourselves by our hands may be shown by the frantic grasp with which a bicycle rider holds on to his handles whenever he feels his balance going. Or again, if when hounds are not running, the reader will station himself on the landing side of a small fence which has to be crossed on the way from covert to covert, he will see how

Pulling Ponies.

many men, who have hunted all their lives habitually, steady themselves by the bridle as they land. Now, if the temptations to supplement the deficiencies of seat by our hands is great in the case of the hunting man, it is far greater in that of the young polo player, who, in his desperate reaches and struggles after the evasive ball, is very likely to try his powers of balance to the utmost.

Any tendency, therefore, to hang on the bridle should be carefully watched and checked at its first appearance. Of too great a trust in the bridle the penalty is assured; of its opposite quality, a hand that guides but never interferes, the reward also is considerable. In the first case you will never have a really first-class pony that is pleasant to ride. Here and there, indeed, an old slug may carry you; and one of those ponies that never pull, simply because they cannot go fast enough, will be your fate, and you may then never hope to play in first-class company, except when the inexorable justice of the slate compels some brilliant Freebooter or regimental captain to endure you on his side in members' games at Hurlingham or Ranelagh. Fast ponies nearly always pull more or less at indifferent horsemen. What I am counselling, however, is not light hands, which are a gift, but a resolute refraining from all use of the bridle, except to guide or restrain. Another fault that is by no means uncommon among young polo players and some

Pulling Ponies.

older ones, is that, as they reach the ball, they catch hold of the pony's head, using the unfortunate animal's mouth as a means to get a purchase from whence to strike the ball. Thus the pony learns to connect the stroke at the ball with pain and inconvenience, and takes not improbably to shying off the ball or galloping over it, tricks that make it quite impossible for his rider to hit it.*

What is needed is that you should form a clear and firm resolution in your mind, not on any consideration to allow yourself to hold on by the bridle. If you do carry this out, not only will you—provided you have a good eye—have a chance of reaching the front rank of polo players, but you will find that you will acquire a very strong seat. "I always thought I could ride a little," said a well-known cavalryman, "but it was only when I went to India with the regiment, and learnt to play polo that I realised how much I had yet to learn. When I came back, and again went out hunting, I found I had better hands and a very much stronger seat on a horse." It is true, indeed, that a strong seat and light hands will make a heavy pocket, since a man who has these two qualifications will mount

---

* Another common fault which may be conveniently noted here is to draw up the leg and drive the heel into the pony on the opposite side to that on which you are hitting. This is done to preserve the balance, but is wrong. The legs should hang straight, and should not follow the movement of the arms and body.

Pulling Ponies.

himself much more cheaply than the man whose hands are indifferent and his seat weak. If you are not one of the mutton-fisted brigade you need not at once reject a pony that pulls. If, indeed, you know of an aminal that is to be sold reasonably and is good-looking and fast, though it pulls a bit, you might watch his owner carefully, and note how he rides, and whether his hands are heavy, and if he rolls much in his saddle. Should you discover these signs, you may reflect that the pony's mouth has been deadened by bad usage, and you may venture to buy him, say for £50. Do not take such a pony out at first into the polo ground, but hack him quietly as you have the opportunity. If he goes fairly well and does not catch hold very resolutely in some crowded place, say Rotten Row in the middle of June, then you may conclude he is not irreclaimable. The polo season, however, is well-nigh over, and he still perhaps hangs on your hand in the game. Then send him down the country, and let him go out to grass for the winter. When springtime comes, and you think of taking him up, let him come up before the others, treat him exactly like a colt come up from grass, and break him carefully all over again. First use the mouthing bit and tackle, then play him quietly in cantering games, and take care at all events that he never goes into a game above himself.

Another pony that seems to pull is the one that

"*BOADICEA.*"

THE PROPERTY OF CAPTAIN SCHOFIELD, R.A.

Pulling Ponies.

is but half exercised, and this is a very common failing. Yet at polo that no pony should ever be above himself is as certain as in the other cases noted above. Arabs are exceptions, for many will play almost as steadily after having been several days in the stable as when they are well exer-

SOMETHING OF A PULLER.

cised. If you have the chance of buying a pony which comes out of a very rich man's stable with something of a reputation as a puller, you may venture upon him for a moderate price, for the presumption is, that it will have been left entirely

Pulling Ponies.

to servants, and will consequently have gone short of exercise. But every man should himself keep a careful eye on his stables, and take care that his ponies are well exercised, that is, that they are trotted out twice a day, five miles out and in, and that they have a couple of hours' walking exercise on the polo days themselves. Many a pony that pulls at first from sheer flightiness and spirits, and hangs on your hand afterwards because he is tired and blown, will go quite kindly if he has regular, constant, and sufficient exercise. No one will deny that a horse in condition pulls much less than a fresh and fat horse, although the former will be galloping easily long after the latter's tail has been twirling round like a barber's brush in a mining village on a Sunday morning. So absolutely indispensable is exercise—and plenty of it—that it would be better even to drive the ponies than to let them be idle, though harness work for polo ponies is not without its drawbacks.

A very considerable experience has shown that in a stable where a large staff is not kept, a tandem is an excellent way of exercising ponies. There is no harm possible to the most precious animal in the lead, and the less-considered pony may be put in the shafts. Captain Whitla, of the Queen's Bays, adopted this plan, and used to exercise his polo ponies by fours in a light drag built for the purpose, with the result that he had some very exciting

Pulling Ponies.

drives when four untried Arabs or country-breds were introduced to four-in-hand at the same time.

I have written much about pulling ponies, but so far there has been no word about bits. Well, I am no great believer in varieties of bits. I am indeed almost inclined to subscribe to the axiom laid down

WRINKLING UP THE CORNERS OF HIS MOUTH.

by a hard-riding friend, viz. : " The horse which I cannot ride in an ordinary double bridle, I cannot ride at all." The proper principle to go on with bits and bridles is, that prevention is better than cure. To this end I would take the greatest pains that the bits used should fit the pony exactly, that the snaffles should be broad, and should not cut or pinch the

Pulling Ponies.

tenderest mouth, that the curb chain be not too tight, and that it be sewn up in wash-leather. Above all, that the bit be in exactly the right place in the pony's mouth. Not one groom in a hundred will take the pains to adjust the bit to the pony, and nothing is commoner than to see the corners of a pony's mouth wrinkled up by the snaffle. This of course should never be, and moreover the bit must be rightly placed. If you cannot see to these points yourself, then let every pony have its own bridle, and let it wear that and no other. But even so, it will be necessary for you to look at the mouth from time to time to see that it is all right.

Among the almost endless variety of bits there are but two which are of much service to the polo player :—

1. The ordinary double bridle with a thicker snaffle than saddlers usually put into them.

2. The Mohawk, a bit for which I do not myself care, but of which such authorities as Captain Daly, Mr. E. Miller, and Sir Humphrey de Trafford speak highly.

The stand-by, however, of an efficient stable is a variety of hunting bridles made to fit each pony. If it be true that there is a key to every horse's mouth, yet it is wiser, if the double bridle in one of its forms be not that key, to leave the task of finding it to other hands Snaffles should not be permitted at polo, for with a snaffle no rider can have proper

Pulling Ponies.

control over his mount. It is necessary at polo not only that you should be able to hold your pony, but that you should be able to collect him and steady him, and a snaffle does not give you that power,

THE ACTION OF A DOUBLE BRIDLE.

whereas the action of a double bridle on a tenderly handled mouth is both rapid and effectual.

Those players who have watched first-rate native teams in India can hardly have helped noticing that their ponies go much less on their shoulders and more on their haunches than English ponies. If a

Pulling Ponies.

pony be put into a school and taught to gallop and turn in a collected manner, with his quarters well under him, he will often cease to pull. This is worth bearing in mind, as hardly any English ponies get the training in this respect, without which no animal would ever be allowed in a game at Patiala or Jodhpur.

CHAPTER XII.

BREEDING POLO PONIES AND THE STUD BOOK SOCIETY.

THE question of breeding polo ponies for the market is one of great difficulty. In fact we have very little experience to go on, for with one exception none of the breeders have ever got beyond the experimental stage. The exception of course is Lord Harrington, who has bred a good many polo and riding ponies, and has met with much success. But even Lord Harrington has not so far established a breed. In spite of the success of "Awfully Jolly" at the stud, it may be doubted whether the blood of this pony will be of equal value in improving the breed of ponies in later generations.

With regard to breeding polo ponies there are two schools of opinion. One party, represented by men like Lord Harrington, Sir H. de Trafford, and Mr. T. Gilbey believe that it will be possible to obtain a breed of ponies for riding and polo which, for the sake of brevity, we will henceforth speak of as polo ponies, which shall breed true to a type. The other party believe that this idea is not a practical one, and that ponies are not so much a separate race as accidents produced by harsh climate and

Breeding Polo Ponies and the

food of an inferior quality. The latter is so far true that all ponies taken up and well fed have a tendency to increase in size. Moreover, this party argues that even if ponies be a distinct breed, however that occurred, yet that they are of no use to us for polo. Granted that there is such a thing as pony character, they say, by which a pony can be readily distinguished from a small horse, we do not want ponies at all. The type at which we aim is not a glorified Exmoor, Welsh, or New Forest pony, but a miniature blood hunter or race-horse, and the best form of this animal is in fact a horse, which for some reason or other has failed to reach the normal height of his race. Pony, they argue, is a misnomer, for the animal wanted at Hurlingham and Ranelagh is not a polo *pony* but a small polo *horse*. Of course, if this view be correct, we must give up all hopes of supplying our polo market from England or Ireland. Such accidents are too infrequent to supply the demand, and we may frankly confess that in this case it is from Arabia, Argentina, America, or Australasia, or all combined that our supply of polo remounts will have to be drawn. This view, of course, cuts away the very ground from under the feet of the Polo Pony Stud Book Society, and condemns their efforts beforehand to disastrous failure.

Before the Polo Pony Stud Book Society made a start the question was a very difficult one. Many

Stud Book Society.

people, however, felt that at all events the experiment proposed by the Society ought to be tried, for, if successful, it must be useful to polo players and might be serviceable to agriculture as opening out a new minor industry for the farm. The idea of the Society was to endeavour to obtain a type and to breed to that. The thoroughbred was to be the foundation of the breed, while the Arab, Barb, Welsh, Exmoor, and other strains were to be introduced.

Certain facts since then have established themselves. The first is that the thoroughbred is the best sire, "Rosewater," so far as I have heard, having beaten every other. There is, too, another good little thoroughbred sire, belonging to Mr. Norris Midwood, "Little Hermit," late "Wanderer." So far the stock of the former do not show much tendency to cast back. Arabs have also been used with varying success. It should be borne in mind that many Arabs in this country are really cross-bred animals of uncertain origin and pedigree, and we know that as a general rule mongrels do not make useful sires. Besides, Arabs have a tendency to get stock bigger than themselves in Europe, and consequently much disappointment has arisen from their use. I have always contended that while an Arab strain has great value both in hunters and polo ponies, it should come through the mare. Our first object

Breeding Polo Ponies and the

must be to get suitable mares for producing polo ponies; English mares with a cross of thoroughbred, Arab and Welsh blood, being my ideal of the future mothers of our Polo Pony Stud. Then, no doubt, by careful and close inbreeding, as in the case of the hackney pony, and with judicious outcrosses to the Arab, and Welsh, or Exmoor, we shall get mares which will give us the class of foals we need; that is, well-bred active little horses, not over 14·2 or under 14 hands. Once the mares are obtained, the rest of the task is easy, and the choice of the horse will be controlled by one or two main considerations, one of which is, of course, that if no stallion like "Rosewater" or "Little Hermit," which are known to get small stock, is available, then to choose an old horse, as such stock has a tendency to run small.

Another point that will have to be most carefully considered is the soil and vegetation on which the mares and foals shall be run. If mare and foal are not sufficiently well done, the latter will be poor, stunted, and weakly. If, on the other hand, the soil be too rich, and the keep too good, it will be impossible to avoid disappointments arising from stock overgrowing the height. It is pretty certain that the happy mean between starvation and luxury can be found, since there are plenty of good ponies, and some counties doubtless will be more successful than others in producing animals of the right size. The conclusion I have come to is that you can get

Stud Book Society.

the type, but that the question of size will be always one that will give trouble, until breeders have discovered, by careful experiment, how to prevent the best of their colts growing over height. Now the Polo Pony Stud Book, if it has done nothing else, has at least done this, that it has shown us we have some excellent mares.

There is one experiment that I should like to see tried. The best small pony in the world is the Burmese.

Alone of small pony breeds it has good bone, while none can beat it in make, shape, endurance, or constitution, and it would, I am sure, be well worth while to import a few choice Burmese ponies, and try the experiment of a cross with our English ponies. We might get for some generations, at all events, the small size without loss either of substance or quality.

Of course polo pony breeding is as yet rather a pastime for men of means than a business. But should the endeavour of the P.P.S.B. Society prove successful then there will be opportunities for breeding ponies for profit. Yet even now it is worth the attention of men who are anxious to turn a penny, to endeavour to breed a good class of pony. This can be done without any great outlay of capital or much risk, by any one who has some land and work for a pony or two. The best way to begin is to pick up a good pony mare with a strain of Welsh

Breeding Polo Ponies and the

blood in her and send her to an old thoroughbred horse. The mare must have more than a dash of true pony blood or the offspring will be too large. Then let the youngster rough it a bit, handle it early in life, but do not work it too soon. Two or three ponies of this class would pay their way. The returns would be nothing very grand, but still in bad times every little helps. If it be possible to get hold of a mare that has herself been a good polo pony so much the better. What I have said may seem scanty and unsatisfactory, but the fact is we none of us know very much about the matter, and can only hope to indicate the possible roads to success in an enterprise which, if successful, will have its full share of prizes to offer.

I have been confronted more than once during the time I have been writing this book, with the possibility that I might have to describe the ideal pony. There were three courses open. To try one's hand boldly, to evade it by saying that ponies go in all shapes—which is partly true—or to say like the profane Australian when the backboard came out of his cart and spilt the load of sand he had laboriously drawn to the top of a high hill, "Boys, I ain't ekal to the occasion." Yet if ever it seemed as if something should be written it is here, when one desires to set before breeders the standard to be aimed at. But no, I think it better to be on the safe side and content myself with a few

Stud Book Society.

words only of general advice on the subject. Bad temper is hereditary, and therefore the disposition of the parents is a thing to be considered. Galloping power and shape is of more importance than substance, and blood more to be considered than bone. For though weight-carrying power is of importance in a polo pony and certainly has its full value in the market, yet it is to be borne in mind that it has only to carry a heavy man for a short time at a stretch and seldom for more than ten minutes. Many well-bred active ponies will gallop for the time required in a game when it would of course fail if asked to do so for a longer period. A heavy man who cannot afford to pay top prices will find himself better carried by well-bred ponies apparently a good deal below his weight than by coarser ponies which seem to have more substance. A well shaped blood-looking galloping pony with a good temper is the thing to aim at, and after that as much substance and power as you can get. The mares to be bought should be of the stamp of "Shylass," or as near to it as possible, since we cannot all hope to obtain pony mares quite of that class. But, after all, as I have already pointed out, a great deal must be left to experiment. We may not all be able to breed polo ponies, but we can all help in the work by joining the Polo Pony Stud Society, which has already made great strides towards solving the problem before us. For two

Breeding Polo Ponies, etc.

years in succession the Society has held shows at Ranelagh and Hurlingham, and what is more important still, it has published three volumes of a stud book which is excellently well edited and arranged, and which will be of the greatest benefit to those who wish to try polo breeding on their own account. I feel sure that those who have studied these volumes will see that if the polo pony can be built up into a separate breed, Mr. Hill and those who have co-operated with him are working in the right direction to do so.

CHAPTER XIII.

Dress and Equipment of the Player.

This is a subject which deserves more attention from polo players than it generally obtains. The Americans have an excellent rule which obliges players always to wear the uniform of the club to which they belong, and what is of real importance is that players should always have some mark to distinguish them from their adversaries. This is for the benefit of the spectators, who cannot follow the game unless they can distinguish the sides. The Rugby jacket is as good a plan as any I know. Sashes are uncomfortable to wear, which is not the case with the sleeveless jackets worn by the Rugby Club. It is much to be desired that each player should wear also a badge distinctive of his position in the game. Mr. Tilney, 17th Lancers, has invented a very ingenious belt, which bears the number of the player, and which should prove useful for this purpose. A simpler plan, however, would be to place round the arms of each player a coloured band distinctive of his place in the team. It would be a great addition to the enjoyment of the spectators if they could tell at a glance where each player ought to be. It would

Dress and Equipment

probably be too much to expect that this should be done in ordinary games, but at all events something of the kind might be arranged at matches.

The choice of polo sticks is a most important matter. However good a player may be he will never do his best unless he gets a stick exactly to suit him. To this end it is necessary to try a good many, for the weight, length, and balance of a stick are matters which affect the play considerably. The length of course will vary with the pony, but not very much, though if you are using ponies of different types, it will be well to hand over to the groom before the match the sticks which suit you best when riding each particular animal. In this case, if an accident occurs, you will have another suitable stick ready at once to your hand. The favourite stick always is the one to go, for the very reason that naturally it has a good deal more use than the others. The wise man looks forward to the future and has a good reserve of sticks always at hand which he can use with comfort. It is a bad plan always to use one stick, for, if you do, you will be quite at a loss when the head flies off, as it is sure to do sooner or later.

In England the square polo head is the best, in India the cigar-shaped one is in most favour. A matter of considerable importance is the angle at which the cane is inserted into the head, and this may be varied with advantage to suit the player. In

of the Player.

fact every man must discover for himself what stick suits him best, and he will find that this alters from time to time. The same pattern will not always be equally useful to the same player. If at any time you find your game going off, it is not a bad plan to try a longer or a shorter stick, or a heavier or lighter head as the case may be. Whippy sticks are dangerous, but on the other hand, stiff canes are bad, as a certain amount of spring is necessary to save the wrist from jar. The finished player will not make use of the same stick he used when he was a beginner, and as a general rule it will be found that a man will incline as he improves in the game to use a shorter and a heavier stick. It will be well to bear in mind Mr. Miller's advice that the handle of a polo stick should be oval and not round. The use of a polo stick, remember, when you have suited yourself, is to hit the ball with, and *not* as a means of rousing your pony. For the latter purpose you should carry a polo whip slung on your left wrist, since sharp spurs are not allowed, either on English or Indian polo grounds. Old ponies do get lazy and cunning sometimes and want rousing, for which purpose the whip is carried. It is well to point out to young players that missing the ball is no reason for hitting the pony. If the pony does not require the whip, then you may as well leave it behind. The probability is that you will in ninety-nine cases out of a hundred be better without it than with it.

Dress and Equipment.

But at all events, one or two sharp cuts will be all that is required. To set to work to flog a pony is as useless as it is cruel and objectionable.

As regards suitable head-dress, it is advisable to wear one of the polo caps designed by Mr. Hardy, and made by Messrs. Barnard of 10, Jermyn Street.* A good cap is a protection to the head and eyes, and though accidents do not often happen through falls in England, blows with the stick are among the chances of the game. The dangers of polo are not great, but nevertheless, it is well to take all reasonable precautions. There are some players, of course, who dislike a cap and prefer to play bareheaded, but though in other matters of play they may be excellent models for our imitation, I should not advise you to copy them in this.

* Since I wrote the above the cap has been lightened without losing its protective power. In my opinion a great advantage.

"*FITZ*" (*First Prize Ranelagh, 1895*).

THE PROPERTY OF CAPTAIN FENWICK, R.H.G.

(*From a picture by Imogen Collier.*)

CHAPTER XIV.

THE EXPENSE AND DANGER OF POLO.

IT is a matter of common opinion that there are two great objections to the game of polo. It is said to be expensive and dangerous. To spend a few words then on considering these two points will not be a waste of space in a book like the present. The expense of polo of course depends very much on the way you set about taking part in the game. Polo in this respect is like hunting. Both are expensive if you set about them extravagantly, neither are beyond the reach of men of very moderate means if a due economy be practised. But our concern here is not with the cost of polo to a rich man, that is entirely a matter between himself and his banker. What I have to try and point out is how little *need* be spent on the game.

First of all let us take the cost of polo to a man who, being stationed in London or bound to town by business, desires to play at one of the London clubs. Supposing he chooses the Ranelagh Club to begin with, which, especially if he is a novice, would be a wise plan, because there he would have the benefit of some useful hints and instruction from the Messrs. Miller. Let us consider what would be the cost of a

The Expense and

season's polo taken at the lowest by a man who had to consider expense. The items would work out somewhat as follows:

	£	s.
Two ponies at £75 each.. ..	150	0
Keep of ditto at club stables, for 12 weeks at £1 1s. per week each	25	4
Journeys from town to club three times a week for 12 weeks at 10s. per diem	18	0
Sticks, saddlery, repairs and sundries	10	0
Club dues	10	10
	213	14
Less sale of ponies at end of season	50	0
	£163	14

Thus the out-of-pocket expenses of a season at polo at one of our best clubs would come to £163. It will be noticed that I have allowed nothing for smokes or drinks, but these items do not belong to the cost of polo. In return for this the player will have kept himself in health and have had a very pleasant time. Then, again, if a man goes to one of the smaller clubs in the neighbourhood of London

Danger of Polo.

the expense will be much less. Deducting from the expenses of the club and journeys about £25 but adding £10 for additional expense in the keep of ponies, the cost would be well under £150. These estimates are of course only approximate, for a man might well give less for his ponies or get more for them when he sells. It will, however, be acknowledged that a polo player need not be a millionaire. In regimental polo of course the expenses are a great deal less than I have quoted. In both cases it may be considered that if a man is playing polo he cannot be doing anything else, and as a matter of fact will not care probably for any other amusements afterwards. A heartily played game at polo leaves one with a pleasant sense of weariness and a disinclination for other pastimes.

Again, in country clubs much less need be spent on the game. The man who lives in the country will probably buy his ponies in the rough at from £35 to £50 a-piece ; he will train them himself, and as he will probably not play them more than twice a week he will be able to use them for his work or for other purposes. Two ponies cost little more than one horse and will do more work. I have always hoped that the day might come when all hunts would have their polo clubs, of which every farmer in the country hunted over by the hounds would be an honorary member, or if, as we can well imagine might be the case, they would prefer to be full members, then that they should join at a very moderate subscription. The ponies might be a source at once of amusement and profit to them. Many a young farmer might play polo who could not hunt; and when once it was realised that good ponies could be found in the country polo clubs, London dealers and players would come down to see what they could buy. Some men would breed, others develop an aptitude for training polo ponies, and both classes would get their fun for nothing. There is nothing among the lesser evils of agricultural depression which strikes me more forcibly than the dulness which hard times have brought to country life. Nothing would be more pleasing in its way than to be able to restore the younger men among the tenant-farmers to the manly exercises and wholesome recreations from which they are now too much cut off. The country polo club would be a social meeting-ground for all classes possessed of similar tastes, for whatever differences of birth or training or association exist they give way before a common love for sport. We have already two such democracies in our midst —the noble equality of cricket and hunting, and the more sordid levelling down of the turf. The expense of keeping up a country club need not be great. Some care of the ground indeed there must be, but the necessary labour might be supplied by the members. No elaborate pavilion is necessary.

Danger of Polo.

A rough, portable stand for spectators, and a tent or movable hut for a dressing room, are all the paraphernalia required. The turf might not be as level or velvety as in the richer clubs; but if a ground be not too uneven, its inequalities will lend variety to polo, and give an opportunity for added skill in the players. I have faith enough in the game to believe that although less luxurious surroundings may add to the difficulties of the game they will in no way detract from its interest.

As to the dangers of polo, they were never very great, and they decrease in inverse proportion to the skill of the players. The causes of accidents are nearly all removable, and are—(1), unmanageable ponies; (2), insufficient or improper bitting; (3), reckless use of the stick; (4), blown ponies, or those which are much under the rider's weight; (5), pure accidents. All except the last two are to be avoided by care and a due sense of responsibility on the part of committees and secretaries of clubs. The rules for the protection of polo players are, with one exception, very clear and sufficient; and if breaches of them are avoided, and kept in check by umpires, the chances of accident will be immensely reduced. There is one rule which I should much like to see adopted in England from the Indian Polo Association Code. I refer to that which ordains that " No player shall at any time place his own stick over, across, or under the body of an adversary's pony."

The practice of stretching across an adversary's pony in front of the fore legs to hit the ball seems to me to be both a dangerous practice and also bad polo. I am strongly in favour of the utmost possible liberty in riding off and hooking the stick, and I entirely dissent from any attempts to do away with those practices. As long as "riding off" is controlled as at present, it adds much to the interest of the game and but little to its danger. There is nothing finer in polo to see, nor anything better to take part in, than one of those grand struggles when two fine teams, magnificently mounted, sweep along under the pavilion at Hurlingham beside the boards, and not one of the eight players perhaps able to hit the ball. Or again, when a great player makes his run in spite of the efforts of one less skilled, but not less determined, than himself to ride him off the ball. This is, of course, only one of the many phases of a game which is rich in variety and therefore in interest. If polo is ever lessened in popular estimation, it need not be by its expensiveness: it certainly will not be by its dangers.

Some peril in all games there must be; but it is merely a common-place to say that this is not a disadvantage, but an absolute necessity. All athletic games are borrowed from the great game of war, and are imitations of the great reality. Some

Danger of Polo.

games derive their chief interests from their copy of tactics, others by the stimulus of conflict or even of danger, but all are indebted to their great prototype for their interests. Polo, perhaps, is borrowed the most directly from the battlefield; it is a lively image of warfare, with no more than just the necessary percentage of danger. So useful is it for a cavalry soldier, that if we had not inherited the game from the Persian warrior horsemen, it might perhaps have been necessary to invent it. The approval of our military authorities has been somewhat hesitating and fitful, it is true, but I do not despair of seeing the day when its value will be recognised by the powers that be, and the regimental polo club be subsidised, as well as the mess and the bands.

CHAPTER XV.

Polo Clubs.

THIS chapter on polo clubs is intended not as an exhaustive account of all the clubs of the world, or even of these in England, but merely as a sketch of some of the best-known among them as a help to the intending player. The headquarters of polo are undoubtedly at Hurlingham, where the members own a fine house and a freehold estate of some fifty acres beautifully placed on the banks of the Thames. That Hurlingham has taken a leading position with regard to polo we owe to the foresight of Captain Monson, the general manager of the club. When pigeon shooting ceased to be the fashionable sport it once was, it seemed for a time that the days of Hurlingham were over. It may be difficult to believe it now; but the time was when the pigeon shooting on a Saturday afternoon at Hurlingham drew crowds as large, as fashionable,—possibly more so—and as interesting as may now be seen on the afternoon of a final of the Inter-Regimental Tournament. About 1872 the tide turned; pigeon shooting was frowned on by some great personages, and ceased to be the fashion. The lawns of Hurlingham were deserted, its membership fell off, few new candidates

Polo Clubs.

came forward. Polo was just then coming into a certain popularity. Whispers were heard of the attractions of the new game, which was then generally known as hockey on horseback. At the same time the Hurlingham House property came into the market. Captain Monson urged his committee to buy it, and the price, £27,000, was raised by debentures and on mortgage. As soon as the purchase was complete, a polo ground was laid out, Captain Smythe became polo manager, and a polo committee was appointed in 1875. The first Inter-Regimental Tournament was played there three years later. The success of this move was immediate. It was in 1875 that a committee consisting of Lords Castlereagh, Valentia, and Churston, Sir Charles Wolseley, Sir Bache Cunard, Captains Herbert and C. Needham, and Messrs. Reginald Herbert, Hugh Boscawen, A. de Murietta, and J. Brocklehurst, drew up that code of rules which has now passed through eleven editions, and the latest of which appears in the Appendix to this work.

The Hurlingham Club has now a large membership, and two excellent grounds. Of course, Hurlingham is something more than a polo club; but the game has been the making of the club which, in its turn, gave polo a helping hand when it hung on a turn of the scales of popularity—whether it should rise to favour or sink back into the obscurity from which it had just emerged. So rapid was the

Polo Clubs.

growth of membership at Hurlingham that Mr. Reginald Herbert soon started a private club at Barn Elms. When he gave up the property the lease was purchased by the committee of the present Ranelagh Club, and a limited company was formed with Mr. Leslie Wanklyn, M.P., Dr. George Hastings, and Mr. C. Lewinger as directors. The club itself

THE PAVILION AT RANELAGH.

was of course managed by the committee, with Lord Dudley as chairman. So well was everything arranged that the Ranelagh Club, with its picturesque club-house and its lovely grounds, at once became a friendly rival to Hurlingham. At Ranelagh polo was a chief attraction, and Mr. J. Moray Brown became the first polo manager, with the present writer as his assistant, who later succeeded

Polo Clubs.

to the sole managership of the club. Then followed Lord Ava and Mr. E. D. Miller, who, as managing director and polo manager respectively, still continue the success which has attended the club from the first. These two clubs are, confessedly, the leading polo clubs of England. They are both conveniently situated for soldiers and others who are obliged to live in or near London, and their Saturdays are crowded with fashionable folk who, having many of them left charming country homes for London, yet are glad to escape from the streets to the shade of the old trees and green turf, velvety with age, of Hurlingham and Ranelagh.

But it is not every one who desires to play polo who can afford the money necessary to those who would play at these clubs. At all events, many men desire to enjoy polo nearer their homes. The Fetcham Park at Leatherhead, the Eden Park at Beckenham, and the Stansted near Bishop's Stortford, are the best-known clubs near London, and at any of these a player will find good management and a good game of polo. Fetcham Park and Stansted have been the schooling ground of many good players, and the latter has the credit of being the home club of Mr. Walter Buckmaster.

Of clubs further away from town Rugby stands first. This club begins play directly hunting ceases in the shires. Then it has an autumn season, which fills up the gap between the close of the London

Polo Clubs.

polo season and the beginning of the hunting. Many enthusiastic players begin at Rugby almost before the last fox of the season has been killed, and from thence they go to London, playing at Hurlingham, or Ranelagh, or both, and then returning to Rugby to finish the season in August and September.

But the most famous ground next to Hurlingham is that of the Phœnix Park Nine Acres at Dublin. This is one of the few grounds which is open to the public free of charge. Polo in Ireland is a most popular spectacle, and the leading players, such as Mr. John Watson and Mr. Jameson, are popular heroes. Although the surroundings of polo in Dublin are of the simplest, and have none of the luxury of Hurlingham or Ranelagh, yet no ground has seen more great matches or been used by a larger number of famous players. Not even at Hurlingham is the play of a higher class than on the Nine Acres in the Phœnix Park. The All Ireland Polo Tournament, and the Irish Inter-Regimental are, with the Inter-Regimental at Hurlingham, the three great matches of the year, and lovers of the game will be amply rewarded for crossing St. George's Channel by the play they will see in either of the first two mentioned.

Edinburgh, too, has a good ground, and has produced some good players. The team winning the County Cup in 1894, Messrs. T. B. and J. Dry-

Polo Clubs.

brough, Mr. Younger, and Captain Gordon Mackenzie, being among the best players, past or present, of this club. The cavalry regiments stationed from time to time at Edinburgh have also taken an active part in the game, and in 1896 the Inniskilling Dragoons sent up a team to the Inter-Regimental which had been playing on the Edinburgh ground, and which was one of the best regimental teams of the year. Although they did not win, there were many who thought they were unlucky not to do so, an opinion in which I agree. Of the other principal towns there are good clubs at Liverpool and Chester.

Besides these English clubs, polo has luxurious homes at some of those delightful American "country clubs" which are the analogue of our Hurlingham and Ranelagh. In Buenos Ayres there is an Argentine Hurlingham named after our English polo head-quarters. Even in far Johannesburg there is a club which has just given evidence of vitality by ordering six dozen polo canes from Mr. Cleave, the cricket bat manufacturer of Birmingham. I had, before the trouble, a kind correspondent at this club, and I thought that the difficulties which overwhelmed that unlucky city had killed out the game just as it was taking root; but it appears that men still forget their troubles in the glow and vigour of a race after the flying ball. There is also a club at Natal.

Polo Clubs.

In Australasia polo clubs are the rule, and not the exception; the three of which I hear the most being those of Sydney, Brisbane, and Auckland. There is a capital and well-edited paper, the *Australasian*, which devotes a considerable space during the season to reporting the games at these clubs.

In India every station has its polo club, and there the game has, as we all know, taken deep root. There is a constant interchange of players between English and Indian polo clubs. Every year officers and others on leave come to share, or at least to watch, the English games, while during the last two years Mr. A. M. Knowles, late 2nd Life Guards Mr. C. E. Rose, R.H.G., and Mr. E. D. Miller have all visited India, and tried their hands at the game there.

In Paris there is a club managed by Mr. Reginald Herbert, where English, Americans, and Frenchmen meet together, bound by their common love of the game. This is, perhaps, the most "International" Polo Club in the world, for no less than four nationalities are represented in its games—French, Spanish, English, and American. Every year the Paris Club holds a most enjoyable tournament in which everything is done that kindness and unlimited hospitality can do to make the visiting teams enjoy themselves. There are polo clubs also at Deauville and Madrid.

A glance at the long list of clubs set forth in the

"NIMBLE."   "CICELY."   "DYNAMITE."   "LADY JANE."

MR. W. H. WALKER'S POLO PONIES.

(After a picture by Adrian Jones.)

Polo Clubs.

Appendix will show how widespread is the game and how quick has been the growth of a sport which in 1872, just twenty-five years ago, was unknown in Europe except to a few Oriental students in the pages of Eastern writers.

CHAPTER XVI.

Recollections and Reflections.

The modern game of polo has already a history, yet it is scarcely twenty-five years since it was first played in England, and much less since it became the interesting and scientific game which it is at the present time. It was in 1879 that I first played polo in India, and it had then only a very limited following. The average height of ponies in use was about 13 hands, though the standard was raised to 13·1 by common consent the following year. The enthusiasts of the game were few, and they were eagerly on the look-out for recruits. I well remember the day I was enlisted in the cause, when, mounted on a perfectly raw pony, I had a stick put into my hands and, as a general principle, was directed to keep on the ball. The most successful players then leaned forward on their ponies and played with a short heavy stick. The ball was dribbled along and taken round, backhanders were almost unknown and not much in favour, for everyone's object was to get the ball and keep it as long as he could without much regard to anyone else. A good many players held the theory that crooking the adversary's stick was bad form. The pace was certainly slow, for it was quite possible to get

Recollections and Reflections.

through an afternoon's polo on one pony, and players only paused when too exhausted to go on any longer. It was difficult to get together eight players for a team with anything like regularity, and when I first played the men were collected from all the services represented in a large station. A civilian, a barrister, a parson, a veterinary surgeon, two gunners, and a policeman were

CROOKED HIS STICK IN THE AIR.

among the most regular players we had. The regiment stationed there looked coldly on our efforts, and none of the subalterns joined us. By degrees, however, the game increased in popularity; the regiment was relieved by the 11th, which had a good polo team, and they in their turn gave place to the 15th, among whom was Mr., now Major, Conran, a very good left-handed player. But it was not till I went to Quetta that I realised the possibilities of the game. In the garrison there

Recollections and Reflections.

were some fine players, three of whom have since reached the front rank in modern polo. These three were Mr. John Watson, Captain Maclaren—then a very junior subaltern—and Captain Capel Cure of the 61st. But, beside these, there were many polo players in the garrison in which were the 13th Hussars, the Scinde Horse, and the 61st and 63rd Regiments. There were, beside, several outside players, of whom the best was Surgeon-Major Fullerton, then—as I believe he is still—the Residency Surgeon. Mr. Watson had not then the form he has now; but anyone could see that, besides being a fine horseman, he was a magnificent hitter, and had a great control over the ball. Even then he was beginning to work at those improvements in the game which have since been associated with his name, and I think we tried him somewhat by our adherence to a more primitive and, I frankly admit now, a far inferior theory of the game. "You can have polo or skittles," he observed once, and he did not leave us in doubt which he considered was the game played by most of us. But we were not unimpressed; and when the end of the Afghan war scattered us to various stations in India, we carried away the ideas we had taken in from Mr. Watson, and put them in practice. The first great change was when players ceased to take the ball round, and backhanders and the present up-and-down game became the rule.

Recollections and Reflections.

Bengal polo was, I think, always a little ahead of the game in Bombay, and when I became associated with the Punjab Frontier Force in 1881 I found the 1st P.C. polo club playing a game very much the same as that now practised, except that the art of combining a side into a whole and thus adding to its force was still somewhat defective. But when, through the kindness of the gallant 1st Punjab Cavalry, I was allowed to join their play, I found a fast and orderly game which was far superior to anything I had seen elsewhere except at Quetta. For three years I was connected with the frontier force, a time on which I can never look back without pleasure, and many pleasant polo experiences date from those years. In the meantime the 10th Hussars, the 9th Lancers, the 8th Hussars, the Gloucestershire regiment, and the greater number of the Cavalry regiments were cultivating the game down-country. From 1877 to 1885 the 9th Lancers and the 10th Hussars divided the honours of the Indian Inter-Regimental Tournament, the 9th, however, winning five times out of seven. In 1886, in the Punjab Tournament, we saw a native team for the first time. For four years the 12th Bengal Cavalry had a team formed of three Sikhs and Captain C. Gough. Of those three native players I am inclined to think that Heera Singh, now a colonel in the Patiala force, was the best player I ever saw. It has been my

Recollections and Reflections.

lot to watch nearly every player of recent years with the fixed attention of one whose duty it is to record their deeds, and I do not hesitate to say that in every department of the game Heera Singh was the best player I have ever seen. Alert, active, and with a certainty of stroke which seemed inevitable in its success, no one ever had greater control of the ball. The only one I can compare to him among our English players of to-day is Mr. Walter Buckmaster, and even he has not the absolute certainty of the great Indian player. In 1891 the Maharajah of Patiala got together his famous team, which consisted of himself and the best men of the 12th B.C. team. When Pretum Singh, Gurdit Singh, the Maharajah and Heera Singh were playing together, mounted on the incomparable ponies which the young Maharajah bought regardless of cost, they formed probably the best polo team that has ever been formed, with possibly one exception. Even so these brilliant native players would probably have held their own against any competitors, as the form of the Patiala men at their best varied less than that of any polo team I have seen. For three years the Queen's Bays, a team which has a splendid record in Indian and Egyptian polo, struggled in vain to wrest the Punjab Cup from the Patiala team. Yet only the 9th Lancers have ever won the Inter-Regimental Tournament more often than

Recollections and Reflections.

the Bays. The Patiala team is not now what it used to be, and it has of late years been more than once defeated by European teams. I imagine from what I hear, though I have not seen them, that the Jodhpur players are the best native team in India to-day.

It is not a little curious that while the best Indian team was running its victorious course, the Sussex County team in England was also showing what could be done by fine combination and mastery over the ball. In his best day Mr. Johnnie Peat was indeed as fine a player as has ever been seen. Of his feats on the celebrated "Dynamite," with which gallant mare his name will ever be associated in the annals of polo, much has been written. It was not till the close of his brilliant polo career that I saw him, and then there was scarcely a team that could extend the three brothers and Mr. Mildmay or Lord Harrington. At last the Freebooters in an ever memorable match in 1895, succeeded in wresting the Champion Cup from the Sussex team after a magnificent game, the result of which was in doubt till the very close. The Freebooters team was so good that under no circumstances could the struggle have been other than an even one. Yet truth compels me to acknowledge that the Messrs. Peat were not, with the exception of Mr. "Johnnie" Peat, at their best on that occasion. Mr. A. E. Peat never was quite the same after his severe illness, and

Recollections and Reflections.

the other brother was not in his best form that day. But allowing for all possible deductions it was a magnificent match, perhaps one of the best, if not quite the best, that has ever been witnessed, even on the Hurlingham ground.

No mention of polo during this period would be complete that did not include Lord Harrington, one of the keenest, most thorough, and most loyal players who ever wielded a polo stick. Himself a fine player he was always kindly and patient with beginners, if only their hearts were in the game, and I think that he scarcely enjoyed a great match more than he did coaching a team of promising youngsters. There is perhaps no man in our time who has exercised a greater and a more beneficial influence on the spirit of the game. Lord Harrington has always been on the side of sport and of fair play. He is characteristically thorough in all he undertakes, and throws almost as much zest into a members' game as into a match. I have no doubt that there is a position in a team which he prefers to any other, but no one could find it out by watching his play, so thoroughly does he strive to do his best for his side, whether he is in the place of Number One, Two, Three, or Back. During the period of which I am now speaking there were three regimental teams contending for supremacy in England and Ireland —the 13th Hussars, the 9th Lancers, and the 10th Hussars. Between the years 1889–1896 the 9th

Recollections and Reflections.

Lancers won the Inter-Regimental Tournament at Hurlingham four times, the 13th Hussars three times, and the 10th Hussars once. And among these matches were some games of unsurpassed interest, for there is never quite the same excitement in any polo match as when it forms part of an Inter-Regimental Tournament. I fear that the 13th Hussars team is for the present a thing of the past. But those who have seen it play will probably agree with me that it was, without exception, the best English "team" they have ever seen. It was not that all the players were of such extraordinary excellence, for only Captain Maclaren is a great polo player, but the perfection of their accord, their discipline, and their training made them the best exponents of scientific polo of the day. The second best team, if second best they be, is probably the team of the Durham Light Infantry, which has recently won the Inter-Regimental Tournament in India for the second year in succession.

It is not my intention here to speak of the polo players of to-day. They are still with us in full activity, and their play can be seen by all. There are Mr. Hardy, Mr. Rawlinson, Lord Southampton, Captain D. St. George Daly, the Messrs. Miller, and that most brilliant player Mr. Walter Buckmaster, in whose performances I take a great delight since first I prophesied his coming excellence when he played for Cambridge against Oxford at Hurlingham

Recollections and Reflections.

in the University Polo Match. Why Cambridge should be such a much better school for polo than Oxford I cannot say. I could wish it otherwise, but so it is. At all events it will be long before Oxford produces such a player as Mr. Buckmaster. The City, too, has given us some fine players of whom two of the best are not so often seen as they were, viz., Messrs. E. B. Sheppard and E. T. Hohler. The latter indeed has sold his ponies and retired from the game.

If, however, we pass from the players to the ponies criticism and appreciation becomes easier. To name the best polo pony I ever saw would be difficult, but if I were forced to make a choice it would be in favour of "The Wig." Many people would put "Dynamite" first, but brilliant mare as the latter is, she is not everyone's mount, and she owed something of her first fame to the partnership between pony and rider when she came out to victory time after time with Mr. J. Peat on her back.

"Skittles," of which there is a sketch in this work, is a mare that I think not far from perfection for galloping under a weight, and her owner, Captain Daly, is not one of the light division. Mr. C. E. Rose's "Yellowman" is a grand pony and absolutely perfect as a player. Another great pony is Sir H. de Trafford's "Gold," though like "Dynamite" this magnificent model of a weight-carrying pony takes

Recollections and Reflections.

some riding at times. But as I think of the ponies I have seen a confusing crowd of good ones comes to my mind: "Elastic," "Elstow," and "Fitz," the grand-shaped winner of many prizes, whose portrait will be found in this book, the team belonging to Mr. W. H. Walker, of Gatacre Grange, Liverpool, and of which the sketch is taken from the excellent picture painted for the owner by Mr. Adrian Jones. "Cicely," "Nimble," "Dynamite" and "Lady Jane" are all four bay mares, and are as good to play as they are to look at, which is saying a good deal. They are indeed about the best team of four ponies in the world at the present moment.

We have seen how polo has grown up from small beginnings in our day, and side by side with the game there has grown, too, a literature. Yet polo has the widest gap in its literature of any sport, for some two thousand years separate the first allusion to the game as played by the Persian princes and the volume of the Badminton Library which was the earliest systematic treatise on it ever written. Then came the bright little book which Mr. Moray Brown wrote, but which did not appear in his life-time, and if there are marks of haste in its composition, and the book is slighter than might have been anticipated, considering the author's great knowledge of the game, it must not be forgotten that it did not have those last touches and

Recollections and Reflections.

the revision which he would doubtless have given it and which could come from no other hand than his own.

Mr. Miller to a great extent filled up the omissions of his friend in his excellent book on "Modern Polo," which may be supplemented by those who come after him, but will never be superseded. Mr. Miller writes with all the force of long personal experience and intimate knowledge of the game, and with a directness and clearness of style which carry home his precepts to the reader. Captain Younghusband, too, has written a book on polo in India which is the standard work in that country, and that, too, is the work of an expert in the game. But in no one's hands has writing on polo reached so high a level as in those of Mr. Brown when he was reporting a great match. These records of the game are worth extracting from the forgotten columns of the paper in which they were published. Sometimes hurried and even careless though they were—for our friend was a hard worker—there is a force and glow in his language and a pictorial power in his descriptions which fairly carry one away. Those who have never played have said that they could understand the game when they read his accounts of great matches. Nor were these vivid descriptions the result of any forced or hireling enthusiasm. To see Mr. Moray Brown reporting a match at Hurlingham

Recollections and Reflections.

was to understand how he got his great knowledge of the game.

To the present writer, to whom, after Mr. Moray Brown's death, fell the duty of reporting polo first for *Land and Water*, and later for the *Field*, it seems as though to watch a match for the purpose of giving an account which shall be intelligible to those who were not present is almost necessary to the full understanding of the game. Indeed, as I have remarked before, as you cannot say everything in the limits allowed, even by the most indulgent editor, the eye must be trained to watch for the turning points of the game, and from the observations made to deduce certain general principles of polo. There are probably only two classes of people who really see a game of polo from beginning to end, and who are able to say why one side won or the other lost, and these are the umpires and the reporters.

I must not omit to mention that in a little known American novel named *Newport*, I recently came across an account of a game of polo, which, though the players are said to skurry after the ball with "the agile inconsequence of kittens," shows that the writer was acquainted with the leading principles of the game. The most fascinating account of a game to be found in fiction is undoubtedly that given by Rudyard Kipling in *The Maltese Cat*, and over this the author has shed the lustre of his genius,

Recollections and Reflections.

though it is probable that he rarely if ever played himself.

Turning from the literature of polo, which has had a resurrection in our own time, after its long sleep of two thousand years or so, it may not be amiss to consider what is the future of the game. Polo is not without powerful foes who urge that it is dangerous, cruel, and expensive. But the only people whose bad word need be feared by the players are the military authorities. They object, not indeed to the game, for its value as a military exercise is most undeniable, but to the expense of tournaments.

Now to be frank, everyone knows that tournaments are as necessary to polo as matches are to cricket, or boat races to oarsmanship. If tournaments were abolished, polo would languish. Let us then for a moment consider the arguments against polo tournaments. It is said that they cause officers to spend too much on ponies, and too little on chargers or hunters. I would not deny that occasionally there has been some truth in the first part of this charge, but it is well known that the two regiments which in our day have been most successful in polo tournaments in England and in India, viz., the 13th Hussars and the Durham Light Infantry, have not paid extravagant prices for their ponies. It is not, however, so well known as it ought to be, that the Hurlingham Committee are most

Recollections and Reflections.

careful to reduce the expenses of those playing in the military tournament as low as possible. A point in favour of the game, which can hardly have escaped the notice of the authorities, is that the officers who stand highest in the polo world are also those who are selected for adjutancies and staff appointments. To take a few well-known instances: Captain Maclaren is now on the Staff and was formerly adjutant of his regiment; Captain Le Gallais, known as one of the best forwards in the army, was adjutant of the 8th Hussars, and has lately been selected for service in the Egyptian Army. Captains Kirk and Whitla, both keen polo players, were successively adjutants of the Queen's Bays, and Major de Lisle occupied the same position in the Durham Light Infantry. There are many other similar instances which could be brought forward.

The plea that polo in England interferes with hunting requires no refutation, for while polo probably never prevented any one from hunting who wished to do so, it has enabled many men to get valuable practice in horsemanship to whom, probably, hunting would have been out of the question. There is on the whole no school of riding to be compared with the polo field for giving strength of seat, power over the horse, and freedom of use to the sword arm. Murmurs may be heard from time to time from those whose ideal of rule, military or civil, is the tyranny of the incapacity of

Recollections and Reflections.

the many over the tastes of the few, but I can never believe that we shall see any overt measures against the game by those rulers who have that "soldierly instinct" to which Lord Roberts refers so often in his most interesting book, and which in an army is necessary alike for those who command and those who obey.

And now my task draws to a close. A labour of love it has been to write this book and to trace the history of a game, the very growth of which is one more evidence if that was needed that the hardihood and chivalry of Englishmen has not degenerated in an age which, though it has sometimes shown a dangerous inclination to imitate the luxury of the later Roman Empire, yet has never copied its softness.

RULES OF POLO.

SOME WINNERS OF TOURNAMENTS.

LIST OF CLUBS.

THE HURLINGHAM CLUB.

Laws and Bye-Laws of Polo, 1897.

RULES AND REGULATIONS.

1.—The height of ponies shall not exceed 14 hands 2 inches, and no pony shall be played either in practice games or matches, unless it has been registered in accordance with the Bye-Laws. Height.

No pony showing vice shall be allowed in the game.

2.—The goals to be not less than 250 yards apart, and each goal to be 8 yards wide. Ground.

A full sized ground should be 300 yards long, by 200 yards wide.

3.—The size of the balls to be 3 inches in diameter. Size of balls.

4.—Each side shall nominate an Umpire, unless it be mutually agreed to play with one instead of two; and his or their decisions shall be final. In important matches, in addition to the Umpires, a Referee may be appointed, whose decision shall be final. Umpire.
Referee.

5.—In all matches for cups or prizes the number of players contending to be limited to four a side. Number of players.

6.—The game commences by both sides taking up their position in the middle of the ground, and the Manager throwing the ball in the centre of the ground. How game commences.

The Hurlingham Club.

Duration of play. 7.—The duration of play in a match shall be one hour, divided into three periods of twenty minutes, with an interval of five minutes between each period.

The two first periods of play shall terminate as soon as the ball goes out of play after the expiration of the prescribed time; any excess of time in either of the first two periods, due to the ball remaining in play, being deducted from the succeeding periods. The last period shall terminate immediately on the expiration of the hour's play, although the ball is still in play.

Exception. In case of a tie the last period shall be prolonged till the ball goes out of play, and if still a tie, after an interval of five minutes, the ball shall be started from where it went out of play, and the game continued as before, until one side obtain a goal, which shall determine the match.

Changing ponies. 8.—As soon as the ball goes out of play, after the expiration of the first ten minutes of each period of play, the game shall be suspended for sufficient time, not exceeding two minutes, to enable players to change ponies. With the above exception, play shall be continuous, and it shall be the duty of the Umpire to throw in the ball punctually, and in the event of unnecessary delay in hitting out the ball, to call upon the offending side to proceed at once. Any change of ponies, except according to the above provision, shall be at the risk of the player.

Bell. 9.—A bell shall be rung to signify the time for changing ponies, and at the termination of each period of play.

10.—An official Time-keeper shall be employed in all important matches.

Goals. 11.—A goal is gained when a ball is driven between the

New Zealand Pony "CHANCE."
THE PROPERTY OF MR. C. E. PUNCHAS (AUCKLAND POLO CLUB).

The Hurlingham Club.

goal posts, and clear of the goal line, by any of the players or their ponies.

12.—If a ball is hit above the top of the goal posts, but in the opinion of the Umpire, through, it shall be deemed a goal. Over top of goal posts.

13.—The side that makes most goals wins the game. To win game.

14.—If the ball be hit behind the back line by one of the players whose line it is, they shall hit it off from the centre of the goal line, between the posts, and all the defending side shall remain behind the line until the ball is hit off, the attacking side being free to place themselves where they choose, but not within twenty-five yards of the ball. This penalty will not be exacted should the ball glance off either a pony or a player. Where ball to be hit from; position of players.

15.—When the ball is hit out of bounds, it must be thrown into the ground by the Umpire from the exact spot where it went out of play, in a direction parallel to the two goal lines, and between the opposing ranks of players. There must be no delay whatsoever or any consideration for absent players. Ball thrown in by Umpire. No delay allowed.

16.—A player may ride out an antagonist, or interpose his pony before his antagonist, so as to prevent the latter reaching the ball, but he may not cross another player in possession of the ball, except at such a distance that the said player shall not be compelled to check his pony to avoid a collision. Riding out an antagonist. Crossing.

If two players are riding from different directions to hit the ball, and a collision appears probable, then the player in possession of the ball (that is, who last hit the ball, or if Definition of Crossing.

The Hurlingham Club.

neither have hit the ball, the player who is coming from the direction from which the ball was last hit) must be given way to. Provided that no player shall be deemed to be in possession of the ball by reason of his being the last striker if he shall have deviated from pursuing the exact course of the ball.

Crooking stick. 17.—No player shall crook his adversary's stick, unless he is on the same side of the adversary's pony as the ball, or in a direct line behind, *and his stick is neither over or under his adversary's pony.*

Off side. 18.—No player who is off side shall hit the ball, or shall in any way prevent the opposite side from reaching or hitting the ball.

Definition of off side. A player is off side when at the time of the ball being hit he has no one of the opposite side nearer the adversaries' goal line, or that line produced, or behind that line, and he is neither in possession of the ball nor behind one of his own side who is in possession of the ball. The goal line means the eight yard line between the goal posts. A player, if off side, remains off side, until the ball is hit or hit at again.

Rough play. 19.—No player shall seize with the hand, strike, or push with the head, hand, arm, or elbow, but a player may push with his arm, above the elbow, provided the elbow be kept close to his side.

Carrying ball. 20.—A player may not carry the ball. In the event of the ball lodging upon or against a player or pony, it must be immediately dropped on the ground by the player or the rider of the pony.

21.—No player shall intentionally strike his pony with the head of his polo stick.

The Hurlingham Club.

22.—Any infringement of the rules constitutes a foul. In case of an infringement of Rules 16, 17, 19, 20, and 21, the Umpire shall stop the game; and in case of an infringement of Rule 18, the Umpire shall stop the game on an appeal by any one of the side which has been fouled. On the game being stopped as above, the side which has been fouled may claim either of the following penalties:— *Penalty for foul.*

(*a.*) A free hit from where the ball was when the foul took place, none of the opposing side to be within 10 yards of the ball.

(*b.*) That the side which caused the foul, take the ball back and hit it off from behind their own goal line.

23.—In the case of a player being disabled by a foul, the side who has been fouled shall have a right to designate any one of the players on the opposite side who shall retire from the game. The game shall be continued with three players a-side, and if the side that causes the foul refuse to continue the game, it shall thereby lose the match. This penalty shall be in addition to that provided by Rule 22. *Penalty for disabling a player.*

24.—Ends shall be changed after every goal, or if no goal have been obtained, after half-time. *Changing ends.*

25.—The ball must go over and clear of the line to be out. *Ball out.*

26.—If the ball be damaged, the Umpire must at once stop the game, and throw in a new ball at the place where it was broken, towards the nearest side of the ground, in a direction parallel to the two goal lines and between the opposing ranks of players. *Throwing in ball.*

27.—Should a player's stick be broken, he must ride to the place where sticks are kept and take one. On no account is a stick to be brought to him. *Broken sticks.*

The Hurlingham Club.

Dropped stick. 28.—In the event of a stick being dropped, the player must pick it up himself. No dismounted player is allowed to hit the ball.

Ground kept clear. 29.—No person allowed within the arena—players, umpires, and Manager excepted.

Accidents. 30.—If any player or pony fall or be injured by an accident the Umpire may stop the game, and may allow time for the injured man or pony to be replaced, but the game need not be stopped should any player fall through his own fault.

Where ball thrown in. 31.—On play being resumed, the ball shall be thrown in, where it was, when the game was stopped, and in the manner provided for in Rule 26.

Disregarding Umpire's decision. 32.—Any deliberate disregard of the injunctions of the Umpire shall involve the disqualification of the team so offending.

Umpire's power to decide all disputes. 33.—Should any incident or question arise that is not provided for in these Rules, such incident or question to be decided by the Umpire.

The Hurlingham Club.

BYE-LAWS.

1.—Every Regiment and every registered Polo Club which is not already represented shall have the right to send one officer or member to represent the Regiment or Club on the Polo Committee, provided that such representatives be members of Hurlingham. *Officers elected to serve on Polo Committee.*

2.—A book shall be kept by the Manager in which all ponies shall be registered with sufficient particulars for the purpose of identification. *Registration of Ponies.*

3.—All ponies which have been played in the Champion, Inter-Regimental, and County Club Tournaments at Hurlingham, the Open Subalterns', and Novices' Tournaments at Ranelagh, and the All Ireland County Cup, and Inter-Regimental Tournaments in Dublin, previous to July 13th, 1896, shall be registered without measurement, provided that an application for registration, accompanied by a certificate, which shall be in the form provided by the Club, and signed by *the person who played the pony* in one of the above Tournaments, be sent to the Manager on or before June 1st, 1897. *Existing Polo Ponies.*

4.—All ponies, other than "existing polo ponies," defined in the preceding Bye-law, may be registered if adjudged not to exceed the prescribed height when measured according to the Rules of Measurement. *Ponies to be measured.*

5.—In order that all members may play during the afternoon, the Manager shall have power to shorten the time, and stop the Match or game at the appointed hour. If a Match is timed to commence at 4, 5.20 shall be the time at which it may be stopped. *Time shortened.*

The Hurlingham Club.

Time. 6.—On ordinary days, in case of a match taking place before the members' game, such match must finish at 5, unless by special leave from the Committee. This does not apply to the tie games in Cup Competitions.

Registration. 7.—All Polo Clubs must be registered with the Manager on May 15th in each year. A Book of Rules and Members of such Club to be forwarded at time of Registration.

Ponies property of Club, &c. 8.—In matches for cups or prizes the ponies must be *bonâ fide* the property of the Club or Regiment contending.

Spurs and blinkers. 9.—No blinkers, or spurs with rowels, allowed except on special occasions when sanctioned by the Committee.

Four players. Precedence. 10.—Not more than four players on each side are allowed to play; the members arriving first at the pavilion to be allowed precedence.

Whistle. 11.—The Umpire shall be required to carry a whistle, which he shall use as required.

Time of ground being opened and hut. 12.—If, in the opinion of the Manager, the ground is in a fit state for play, it shall be opened for not less than six players, at 3 o'clock each day, Fridays excepted, when the ground is closed. Each set of players shall be allowed the use of the ground for 20 minutes. All play shall cease and the ground shall be cleared by 7.15 p.m.

Colours. 13.—The colours of the Hurlingham Club shall be light blue shirts. The second colours white and red. In members' matches every player shall wear a white shirt or jersey, the sides being distinguished by red and blue waistcoats, supplied by the Manager.

The Hurlingham Club.

RULES OF MEASUREMENT.

1.—The measurement shall be made by an Official Measurer under the supervision of the Polo Committee. Such Official Measurer shall be appointed by the Committee and shall be a duly qualified Veterinary Surgeon. Official Measurer.

2.—The Official Measurer shall attend for the purpose of measuring ponies on the first day in the season on which the ground is open for play, and on certain subsequent days which shall be advertised in due course. Time of measurement.

3.—The person presenting a pony for measurement shall fill up and sign a form, supplied by the Club, containing particulars and a description of the pony, and shall pay to the Manager a fee to be fixed by the Committee before the pony can be measured. Description of pony to be signed, and fee paid.

4.—Ponies aged 5 years and upwards may be measured and registered for life; ponies under 5 years can be registered for the current season only. The Official Measurer shall determine the age of the pony. Age of pony.

5.—A pony shall not be measured if he appears to have been subjected to any improper treatment with a view to reduce his height, or if he is in an unfit state to be measured. If a pony is rejected under this Rule, he shall not be presented again for measurement until the following season. Condition of pony.

6.—The measurement shall be made with a standard approved by the Club, and in a box with a level floor specially erected for the purpose. Standard and place of measurement.

The Hurlingham Club.

HURLINGHAM CLUB.
Form for Description of Pony presented for Measurement.

Owner's Name.	Pony's Name.	Colour.	Sex.	Age.	Distinctive Marks.

Date

Signature of Owner

The Hurlingham Club.

7.—Neither the owner of the pony nor his servant shall on any account enter the box during the measurement, nor shall any other person be admitted unless specially authorized by the Official Measurer, but members of the Polo Committee shall have a right to attend the measurement when their own ponies are not being measured. *Access to measuring.*

8.—The pony shall stand stripped on the level floor, and the measurement shall be made at the highest point of the withers. *Position of pony and standard.*

9.—The pony shall be held by a person deputed by the Official Measurer. *Holding pony.*

10.—The head shall be so held that a line from the poll to the withers would be parallel to the floor. *Position of head.*

11.—The forelegs from the point of the shoulder, and the hind legs from the back downwards, shall be as perpendicular to the floor and as parallel to each other as the conformation of the horse allows. *Legs.*

12.—The wither may be shaved, but the mane must not be pulled down, or the skin of the neck or wither in any way interfered with. *Hair and skin.*

13.—Ponies may be measured with or without shoes, but no allowance shall be made. *Shoes.*

14.—Any person who is dissatisfied with the determination arrived at may by a written application, presented to the Manager within seven days from the time of measurement, apply for a re-measurement. Such re-measurement shall take place in the presence of two members of the Polo Committee, and on the first convenient day which may be appointed, and their decision shall be final. *Appeal.*

The Hurlingham Club.

REVISED RULES FOR COUNTY CLUB CUP.

(OPEN TO ALL REGISTERED COUNTY CLUBS.)

1.—All Polo Clubs must be registered with the Manager on May 15th in each year. A Book of Rules and Members of such Club must be forwarded at time of registration, and no player is eligible to play for his Club in the County Cup unless his name appears on such list of Members.

2.—Any Member playing for his Club must be a resident in the county where such Club has its ground, or reside within 50 miles of the Club ground.

No player is eligible to play for his Club unless he has played on at least six different days on the Club ground during the past season, or on six different days during the present season, in Club games or matches.

3.—The team which has played for the Open Cup, and won the same during the last three years, is not eligible to contend, and not more than one player of such a team may play in the same team for his Club.

4.—Any players eligible to play for their universities in the inter-university match may play for Oxford and Cambridge University Clubs, provided that they fulfil the necessary qualifications in other respects.

5.—A residence within the Metropolitan area of London cannot act as a qualification for any Club.

6.—Ranelagh and Hurlingham are not eligible to contend.

7.—The fact of an officer being quartered in the neighbourhood does not constitute a residential qualification; with

The Hurlingham Club.

the exception that an officer with a militia, volunteer, yeomanry, or staff appointment for not less than three years, and who has not played for his regiment in the Regimental Tournament of the same year, is eligible to play for his Club.

8.—Entries to be made in writing to the Manager at least ten days previous to the date fixed for the first game, giving the names and addresses of each player. And a certificate must be furnished by the Captain or Secretary of the Club at the same time that the necessary conditions as to qualification have been fulfilled by all the players entered. The Manager shall not accept an entry from any Club, unless it is registered according to Rule 1.

9.—The Captain of each team on entering to deposit Five Pounds with the Manager, which shall be returned on the Tournament concluding. Should the team be scratched, the Five Pounds shall be forfeited and go to the team which is second.

10.—In the event of one of the players being prevented from playing for some reason that the Polo Committee may consider *bonâ fide*, they may allow another man, a member of the same Club, and properly qualified, to be nominated in his place; such substitute cannot be taken from a team entered for County Cup unless the same is scratched.

11.—The ponies played must be *bonâ fide* the property of a member of the Club.

12.—The decision of the Hurlingham Committee on any point is final.

The Hurlingham Club.

CONDITIONS FOR CUP TOURNAMENTS.

Champion Cup Conditions.

Open.   1.—Open to any Polo Teams.

2.—The number of players on each side is limited to four.

Entry form.   3.—The entries, naming colours, to be made on or before 5 p.m., on the Saturday prior to the week of competition.

Draw.   4.—The respective Teams to be drawn, and the said draw to take place on Saturday, at 5 p.m., prior to the week of competition.

Name Players.   The Captain of each Team to name his four players at time of entry.

Substitutes.   5.—In the event of one of the players being prevented from playing from some *bonâ fide* good reason, the Polo Committee may, if they think fit, allow another man to be nominated in his place; such substitute must not, however, be taken from among the players selected in any other Team.

Three teams.   6.—Unless three Teams contend the Cup will not be given.

Tie.   7.—In case of a Tie between two Teams, it must be played off the same day till one Team obtain a Goal, always excepting both Teams electing to postpone.

INDIAN POLO ASSOCIATION RULES.

RULES FOR THE REGULATIONS OF TOURNAMENTS, &c.

1.—The new rules for the measurement of ponies shall have effect from the 1st April, 1893. The maximum height of polo ponies shall be thirteen hands and three inches.

2.—All tournaments played under the Rules of the Indian Polo Association shall be under the management of three Stewards, who shall be elected locally.

3.—There shall be a right of appeal to the Stewards upon all questions which are not by these Rules declared to be subject to the final decision of some other authority, such as umpires, &c., and the decision of the Stewards in all such appeals shall be final.

4.—Any question which may arise in the course of a Tournament, and which is not provided for by these Rules, shall be referred for decision to the Stewards, who may, if they think fit, refer the matter to a Committee of three members of the Indian Polo Association, whose decision shall be final. This Committee to be selected annually at the General Meeting.

5.—The duration of play, and the number of ponies allowed to be played by teams in a tournament, shall be decided locally, provided that the maximum duration of play in any match does not exceed forty minutes, exclusive of stoppages.

Indian Polo

6.—There shall be an annual meeting of Members of the Indian Polo Association during the Inter-Regimental Tournament. No alteration in the rules or constitution of the Indian Polo Association to be made except at this meeting; due notice having been given to all members by the honorary secretary. Every subscribing member may have a vote. Voting by proxy is permitted.

7.—It shall be left to the discretion of the Committee appointed under Rule 4 to grant permission for Measuring Committees, consisting of three or more members, to be held at such Tournaments as they may consider desirable. Application for such Measuring Committee, which must be accompanied by the names of the proposed members, none of whom should be intended players in the Tournament without special sanction of I.P.A. Committee, must be made to the Honorary Secretary, Indian Polo Association, at least one month previous to the commencement of the Tournament.

8.—Ponies when once measured in accordance with the rules laid down by the Indian Polo Association may be given Life Certificates by the Association. Racing certificates will now be accepted. Certificates granted to ponies under six years old will be available for the current season only.

9.—The Measuring Committee, which has been sanctioned under Rule 7, shall measure all ponies which are intended to be played in the Tournament, provided they do not already hold life or season certificates. The list of ponies, any team intends playing, must be submitted to the Measuring Committee at the time of measurement, and on the conclusion of the Tournament a certificate will be furnished by each team to the Honorary Secretary of the Tournament that the ponies measured and passed by the Measuring Committee have

Association Rules.

actually played in the Tournament. This will be forwarded with the register mentioned in Rule 16 to the Secretary. Indian Polo Association Certificates will not be granted to ponies that, though measured, have not played in the Tournament.

10.—No pony shall play in a Tournament unless—

(*a*) it has got a Life or Season Certificate ;

(*b*) it has been measured and passed by the Committee. Such Committee to assemble at the Station where the Tournament is held, within one week of such Tournament. The Honorary Secretaries of Tournaments will advertise in a daily newspaper, published in the province in which the place is situated, the date of assembly of such Committee. Not less than seven days' notice shall be given. Any team knowingly playing any pony in a Tournament which has not been measured in accordance with Rule 9, or which is not in possession of an I.P.A. Certificate, shall be disqualified for that Tournament.

11.—The inspection of ponies shall take place during the week previous to the commencement of the Tournament.

12.—Any two of the persons empowered under Rule 9 shall form a quorum for the purpose stated ; and if more than two act, the decision shall be that of the majority.

13.—If, after the publication of the notice referred to in Rule 10, the necessary quorum cannot be obtained owing to the inability of any person to attend or act, the Stewards of the Indian Polo Association may appoint a substitute for such person.

14.—No person shall take any part in ageing or measuring his own pony or a pony in which he has an interest.

Indian Polo

15.—The person presenting a pony to be aged or measured shall fill up and sign a form containing such particulars as the Stewards of the Indian Polo Association shall from time to time direct. The following shall be the Form :—

Owner.	Colour.	Class.	Sex.	Name.	Remarks.

*Signature*_____

*Date*_____

*Place*_____

16.—When the age or height of a pony is determined, the name, colour, and distinguishing marks of such pony, as well as his age and height, shall be entered in a register kept for the purpose; and the entry as regards such pony shall be signed by all the persons who have taken part in the determination. If the entry is made in a register which is not kept by the Secretary of the Indian Polo Association, the sheet containing it shall be forwarded to the said Secretary without delay, and shall be filed in the office of the Indian Polo Association, and inserted in the Polo Calendar.

17.—Any person who is dissatisfied with the determination arrived at may, by written application presented within three days, apply for another determination. A note of application

Association Rules.

shall be made in the register referred to in Rule 16; and if the pony is presented at a time and place of which due notice shall be given, he shall be again aged or measured, as the case may be. The particulars of the second determination shall be entered in the register above mentioned, and the determination shall be final. If the pony is not presented at the time and place fixed, the original determination shall hold good, unless the Stewards of the Indian Polo Association direct otherwise.

18.—A pony shall not be measured if he appears to have been subject to any improper treatment with a view to reduce his height, or if he is in an unfit state to be measured, and he shall not be aged or measured if he is unnamed, or if all the particulars required under Rule 16 are not furnished. If a pony is rejected on the ground that he has been subjected to improper treatment, the persons before whom he is brought may order that he shall not be again presented within a period of six months.

19.—For every pony presented to be aged or measured, there shall be paid in advance a fee of Rs.2. Such fee will be collected by the Honorary Secretary of the Tournament where the Measuring Committee is held and credited by him to the Indian Polo Association.

20.—Any person may, on payment of a fee of R.1, obtain from the Secretary of the Indian Polo Association a certified extract of an entry in the register referred to in Rule 16.

21.—The following rules shall be observed in measuring ponies :—

(i.) The pony shall stand stripped on a perfectly level platform, and the measurement shall be made at the highest

Indian Polo

point of the withers with a measuring rod of a pattern approved by the Stewards of the Indian Polo Association.

(ii.) He shall be held by a person deputed by the persons conducting the measurement, and he shall not be touched by any one else without their permission.

(iii.) The head shall be so held that a line from the poll to the wither would be parallel to the platform.

(iv.) The fore legs from the point of the shoulder, and the hind legs from the back downwards, shall be as perpendicular to the platform and as parallel to each other as the conformation of the horse allows.

(v.) The wither may be shaved, but the mane must not be pulled down or the skin of the neck or wither in any way interfered with.

(vi.) No allowance shall be made for shoes.

(vii.) Not more than five minutes shall be allowed for the measurement.

22.—In ageing ponies a veterinary surgeon shall, if possible, be consulted.

23.—In case of the number of entries for any Tournament not being a power of 2 as 4, 8, 16, &c., all byes shall be in the first round. For instance, 13 teams enter, 3 draw byes, the remainder play off, leaving 8 to play in the second round.

24.—Each team to consist of not more than four players.

25.—Native teams may be admitted as Honorary Members of the Indian Polo Association without voting powers.

26.—All Station, Regimental and Battery Polo Clubs can become members of the Indian Polo Association on payment of a donation of Rs.5.

Association Rules.

27.—The Polo year shall be considered to be rom the 1st April in any one year to the 31st March in the following year. Any alteration in these rules, as well as those of the game, made in accordance with Rule 6, shall have effect from the commencement of the new Polo year.

28.—A Polo Calendar shall be published annually in June, under the authority of the Indian Polo Association.

Indian Polo

RULES OF THE GAME.

1.—Each match shall last for not more than forty minutes, to be divided into eight periods of five minutes actual play. When the ball is out of play, time is not to count, but the ball must be revived at once, and players cannot ride off the ground as heretofore except at their own risk.

2.—When starting the game on reviving the ball from the time the Umpire may throw in the ball mounted or else depute a bystander to do so.

3.—In the event of a tie the goal flags shall be placed forty-four feet apart, and the game shall be immediately started as directed in Rule 18.

Play to continue for five minutes, when time shall be called, unless the game is still a tie, in which case play shall be continued until one side gets a goal.

4.—No team shall be compelled to play on two consecutive days, except in the case of a tie.

5.—Three minutes' interval shall be allowed after every period, it being optional, if both sides agree, to have no interval; but three minutes must not be exceeded.

6.—The Stewards shall nominate two Umpires and four Goal Referees for each match. Those selected as Umpires must be regular Polo players, and must possess a thorough knowledge of the game. In the event of the Umpires seeing a player infringing these Rules, as herein laid down, when the ball is in play, it shall be their duty to stop the game, whether appealed to or not, and the penalties laid down in Rules 40 and 41 shall be enforced.

Association Rules.

7.—The Umpires shall have the power of ordering off the ground any player who, after having been warned, plays unfairly or rides dangerously, and it shall be their duty to do so. Umpires shall order any player cutting his pony with sharp spurs to remove them or to use spurs without rowels. Such player shall not be replaced.

8.—Each Umpire shall be provided with a whistle, the blowing of which by either Umpire is a sign that the game is to stop till the decision is given.

9.—The Umpires shall order off the ground any pony which they may consider dangerous or improperly bitted, or which the rider has not under thorough control.

9(a).—In order to be able to discharge their duties properly, Umpires must be mounted on well-trained and fast ponies, so as to be able to ride near enough to the ball to give a decision at any moment, and yet not to interfere with the players.

10.—The Umpires shall have the power of ordering play to begin after the time fixed, notwithstanding the absence of any player.

10(a).—In the event of an accident, the Umpires are empowered to stop the game.

11.—The decision of the Umpires shall be final on all questions declared by these Rules to be subject to their final decision, and shall also be final on all questions arising out of the actual play of the game, except on questions arising out of Rules 36 and 37, on which questions the Umpires shall have no voice.

12.—The decision of the " Goal Referees " standing at the goal in question, shall be final as to whether the ball has passed between the goal flags or subsidiary goal marks. If

Indian Polo

appealed to by the Umpires, their decision shall also be final as to whether the ball has passed over the back line.

13.—The size of the ground shall be as nearly as possible 300 yards long and 200 broad, and shall be marked off by flags.

14.—At each end of the ground, in the centre of the back line, there shall be a goal marked by flags, which shall be 22 feet apart. The line between the goal posts shall be called the goal line.

15.—Sides shall toss for choice of goals.

16.—Goals shall be changed after goal obtained. Should the game continue for two periods without a goal being obtained, goals shall be changed and the game again started from the centre of the ground; but should any goal afterwards be obtained, goals shall be changed after that goal, and after any subsequent goal without reference to time.

17.—The ball shall be of bamboo root, about ten and a-half inches in circumference, and four ounces in weight.

18.—To start the game, and after each goal, the ball shall be thrown into the centre of the ground by a person dismounted who shall be deputed by the Umpires to do so; the two sides ranging themselves opposite each other, not nearer to the side line than a point which shall be marked 80 yards from it, the ball always to be thrown in from the same side of the ground.

19.—The ball on being hit out at the side line shall be thrown in under hand, as soon as possible, by one of the Umpires, or by any one deputed by him to do so, in a straight line at right angles to the line and as hard as possible—the ball to touch the ground before passing the side line. The ball shall be considered to be in play as soon as it crosses the

Association Rules.

side line, unless the Umpire should immediately call it back. The Umpire shall be the sole judge as to whether the ball is properly thrown in or not. The thrower is to be on foot.

20.—If the ball is hit behind the adversary's back line by one of the opposite side, it shall be hit off, by one of the side whose line it is, from a spot as near as possible to that at which it crossed the line. None of the opposite side shall stand within thirty yards of the line until the ball is hit off.

21.—If the ball is hit behind the back line by one of the side whose line it is, it shall be hit off from the nearest corner by one of the opposite side; no other player of that side shall stand within thirty yards of the back line until the ball is hit off; and all the players of the side behind whose back line the ball is being hit, shall stand behind their own back line.

The above rule shall be enforced at the option of the side who have the right to hit off from the nearest corner. If they decline to enforce this rule, the ball shall be hit off according to Rule 20, excepting that the side from whose back line the ball is being hit off shall stand behind their own back line.

22.—The ball shall be considered to have been hit off when it has been hit across the back line with the intention of hitting off.

23.—Small flags shall be placed on the side lines to mark fifty yards and thirty yards from the back line, and a section of a circle shall be marked off at each corner of the ground with the corner for the centre and a radius of five yards.

24.—No unnecessary delay shall take place in reviving the ball under Rules 19, 20 and 21. Any necessary delay shall not count as actual play.

25.—No player shall cross or ride dangerously.

Indian Polo

26.—If two players are riding to hit the ball from different directions, and a collision appears probable, the player not in possession of the ball must give way to the player in possession of the ball. The player who hit the ball last, or who has come in the same direction as the ball did when last hit, is in possession of the ball.

27.—No person other than the Umpires and players shall come on the ground while the ball is in play.

28.—"Riding off" is permitted. "Hustling" is not. The penalty for hustling shall be the same as that for dangerous riding.

The following is a general definition of "riding off":—

28 (a)—A player shall be considered to "ride off" fairly, when, having placed himself abreast of an adversary (after following a line of direction as nearly as possible parallel to that in which his adversary is moving), he gradually forces him from, or prevents his continuing in, the direction in which he is riding. This definition to be considered together with Rule 25 on "crossing."

(b) In so "riding off" a player shall be permitted to use his arm between the shoulder and the elbow, provided the elbow be kept close to the side.

(c) Any other attempt to "ride-off" shall be "hustling."

(d) Players must not play left-handed.

29.—If any player catch the ball in any way during the game, it must be dropped on the ground at once.

30.—Subject to the next Rule, a player may crook, or stop an adversary's stick, when the adversary is about to strike the ball.

Association Rules.

31.—No player shall at any time place his own stick over, across or under the body of an adversary's pony. No player shall crook his adversary's stick unless he is on the same side of the adversary's pony as the ball, or immediately behind.

32.—No player, when "off-side," shall be allowed to hit the ball, or in any way interfere in the game, intentionally or otherwise; should he do so, the penalty of foul can be claimed.

33.—No player, who is "off-side," shall hit the ball, or shall in any way prevent the opposite side from reaching or hitting the ball. A player is "off-side" when, at the time of the ball being hit, he has no player of the opposite side nearer the adversaries' goal line or behind that line, and he is neither in possession of the ball nor behind one of his own side, who is in possession of the ball. The goal line means the right yard line between the goal posts. A player, if "off-side," remains "off-side" until the ball is hit or hit at again.

34.—No dismounted player shall be allowed in any way to take part in the game while dismounted.

35.—When the game is stopped owing to an accident or broken ball, the umpire shall revive the game by throwing in a ball at the spot where it was when the accident occurred, or where it was last struck when the ball broke.

36.—A goal is obtained if the ball be hit between the flag-posts of the goal; or if it be kicked by a pony between the flag-posts of the goal; or if being hit higher than the top of the posts it would, in the opinion of the Goal Referee, have gone between the posts produced; or, if it be hit over the

Indian Polo

goal line between the two points where the goal posts should stand, when either or both of the goal posts shall have been displaced. The ball must go over and clear of the line to count as a goal.

37.—A subsidiary goal is obtained in the same way as a true goal, except that to score a subsidiary goal, the ball must pass between the subsidiary goal mark and the goal post which is nearest to it.

The subsidiary goal marks must be shown on the ground by a white line, and not by flags.

Subsidiary goals are to be measured eleven feet from each goal post on the outside—the sum of the subsidiary goal thus equals the true goal. No number of subsidiary goals will ever equal a true goal. In the event of a tie in the actual number of goals, the side scoring the greater number of subsidiary goals will be considered the winner.

38.—No goals or subsidiary goals shall be counted which have been obtained by unfair play.

39.—Any infringement of the Rules constitutes "unfair play" or "a foul."

40.—In case of "a foul," other than crossing or dangerous riding, being declared, the Umpire shall stop the game, and either of the two following penalties may be claimed by the side which has been declared to have been fouled:—

(a) A free hit from where the ball was when the "foul" occurred, and none of the opposite side to be within ten yards of the ball. But if the "foul" occurs near the goal of the side which causes the "foul," a free hit shall be given from a spot not within thirteen yards of the goal, but as near as possible to where the "foul" occurred.

"STONECLINK."

Association Rules.

(*b*) That the side which caused the "foul" take the ball back and hit it off from behind their own back line, and they shall stand behind their back line until the ball is hit off.

41.—The following shall be the penalty for crossing or dangerous riding :—In the event of a "foul" being given for crossing or dangerous riding, the following shall be the penalty :—A free hit from a spot fifty yards from the back line of the side causing the "foul" and as nearly as possible opposite the spot where the "foul" took place, unless the "foul" takes place less than fifty yards from the back line, in which case the free hit shall be given from the spot where the "foul" occurred; none of the side causing the "foul" may stand between the flags, nor may they ride out to meet the ball through the goal. When a foul is given, the period shall not come to an end until the penalty shall have been enacted.

Indian Polo Association Rules.

STATION POLO.

1.—In every station where Polo is played, their players shall elect a Committee of their members to be called the "Station Polo Committee."

2.—The duties of the Station Polo Committee shall be to regulate all matters in the station connected with Polo, to see that the station games are played in accordance with the Indian Polo Association Rules, and to stop at once any tendency to dangerous or foul riding.

3.—With this object they will inspect and measure every pony before it is allowed to play in a practice game. Such measurements are only valid for station games. All ponies before playing in a Tournament must be re-measured. No pony will be allowed to play except it be well broken, properly bitted, and under the maximum height.

4.—They will also prevent any player from taking part in a fast game, who from ignorance of the Rules or from indifferent horsemanship is likely to be a source of danger on the Polo field.

5.—The Committee will also see that, whenever possible, an Umpire is appointed for every practice game; in the event of no one being available for this duty, the Back on each side shall be given the authority of an Umpire in matters which do not affect him personally.

AMERICAN POLO ASSOCIATION.

1.—The Polo Association shall consist of an Association of Polo Clubs, each to be represented by one delegate, who shall out of their number elect at the Annual Meeting a Committee of five for the term of one year.

2.—To have the entire control of all matters relating to the Polo Association, and shall be the authority for enforcing the rules and deciding all questions relating thereto. They shall have the power to appoint all officials for a term not exceeding their own, and to make such changes in the rules and bye-laws as they may consider necessary. The Chairman of the Association shall be a member of the Committee *ex-officio*.

3.—Every Club and its delegate up for election shall be proposed and seconded in writing by two delegates, and the election may take place at any meeting of the Committee. The election to be determined by ballot. One black ball in five to exclude. When any Club shall withdraw its delegate, his successor shall be proposed, seconded, and voted for, in like manner.

4.—Each Club a member of the Association shall pay an annual subscription of $50.00. All subscriptions shall become due, and payable in advance, on April 1st of each year. The subscription remaining unpaid after the 1st of June, is to be considered as in arrear, and no Club whose subscription is in arrear shall enjoy any privileges of the Association, nor take part in any games with members in good standing.

American Polo Association.

5.—The Annual Meetings of the Association shall be held on the second Tuesday in March, at such place in New York City *as the Committee* may designate. The Committee shall meet once a month or oftener, from April to September inclusive. Three members to constitute a quorum at the Committee meetings.

6.—In the absence of a Club delegate the President or Secretary of such Club may furnish a written proxy to be used at the meeting for which it is named.

7.—Minutes of the proceedings of every meeting shall be taken during their progress by the Secretary; or, in case of his absence, as the Chairman shall direct, and be afterwards copied into a Minute Book, to be kept for that purpose, and, after being read at the next meeting, shall be signed by the Chairman of that meeting.

8.—The order of business at the Annual Meetings shall be as follows:—

(1) The noting of the members present.

(2) Reading of minutes of last annual meeting, and of subsequent special meetings.

(3) Reports of Treasurer and other officers.

(4) Reports of Special Committees, and consideration of any resolutions attached thereto.

(5) Election of officers.

(6) Deferred business.

(7) New business.

The order of business may be suspended, on motion, by vote of two-thirds of the members present.

9.—In case the conduct of a delegate be considered injurious to the character or interests of the Association, in the opinion of any five members, who shall certify the same

American Polo Association.

in writing to the Committee, a meeting of the Committee shall be held to consider the case.

If the member whose conduct is in question shall not explain the same to the satisfaction of the Committee, or if the Committee acting as Judges shall be of the opinion that the member has committed a breach of the Rules of Polo, or of the Bye-Laws, or been guilty of conduct injurious to the interests of the Association, which ought not to be condoned, they may call upon such member to resign ; or shall request the Club whose representative he is to withdraw him, and nominate his successor for election, and in event of their neglecting to do so, the Committee shall have power to expel him, and his Club shall be erased from the list of members ; provided, always, that such expulsion shall only be by a majority of two-thirds, at a Committee Meeting consisting of not less than five members.

In any case where the expulsion of a delegate is deemed necessary, the decision of the Committee shall be without appeal, and the Club so expelled shall have no remedy against the Committee.

10.—A delegate may issue free tickets of admission to members of the Club he represents, good for one week at any Club ground during Association week there.

American Polo Association.

RULES OF THE AMERICAN POLO ASSOCIATION.

Revised April, 1894.

1.—The grounds to be about 750 feet long by 500 feet wide, with a 10-inch guard from end to end on the sides only.

2.—The height of the ponies must not exceed 14 hands and 1 inch.

3.—The balls to be of Bass wood, with no other covering than paint, $3\frac{1}{8}$ inches in diameter, and not to exceed 5 ounces in weight.

Mallets to be such as are approved by the Committee.

4.—The Goal Posts to be 24 feet apart, and light enough to break if collided with.

5.—Match games between pairs shall be two periods of fifteen minutes each, actual play. Time between goals and delays not counted; two minutes after a goal has been made and five minutes between periods for rest, unless otherwise specified.

6.—Match games between teams of three shall be four periods of fifteen minutes each, actual play. Time between goals and delays not counted; two minutes after a goal has been made and five minutes between periods for rest, unless otherwise specified.

7.—Match games between teams of four shall be three periods of twenty minutes each, actual play. Time between goals and delays not counted; two minutes after a goal has been made and ten minutes between the periods for rest, unless otherwise specified.

American Polo Association.

8.—Each team to choose an umpire, and, if necessary, the two umpires to appoint a referee, whose decision shall be final.

9.—Each team should have a substitute in readiness to play when a match is on.

10.—There shall be a captain for each team, who shall have the direction of positions and plays of his men. The home captain shall provide two acceptable goal judges, whose decisions shall be final, in regard to goals made at the end at which each may be placed.

11.—No captain shall allow a member of his team to appear in the game otherwise than in his Club uniform.

12.—Only players, umpires and referee allowed upon the ground during the progress of the game.

13.—The game to begin when the ball is thrown between the contestants, who shall be in line facing each other in the middle of the field, unless it is agreed between the captains to charge. The charge to be from a line 30 feet in front of the goal posts. When the signal to charge has been given the first and second players must keep to the left of the ball until it has been hit.

14.—It is forbidden to touch an adversary, his pony, or his mallet, with the hand or mallet during play, or to strike the ball when dismounted. A player shall not put his stick over his adversary's pony either in front or behind. In "riding off" or "hustling," a player shall not push or strike with his arm or elbow.

15.—In case of an accident to a player or pony, or for any other reasonable cause, the referee may stop the game, and time so lost shall not be counted. When the game is

American Polo Association.

resumed the ball shall be thrown between the players, who shall be lined up at the point at which the ball stopped. But if the game is stopped on account of a foul, the ball is to be thrown in at the place at which the foul occurred.

16.—When the limit of time has expired, the game must continue until the ball goes out of bounds, or a goal is made, and such overtime shall not be counted.

17.—In event of a tie at the end of the last period, the game to be continued until one side is credited with a goal or part of a goal.

18.—When the ball goes out of bounds at the sides, it must be thrown in from the place at which it went out, by the Referee, or by an impartial person, between the two sides, which shall be drawn up in line facing each other. When the ball goes out ends, the side defending that goal is entitled to a knock out from the point at which it crossed the line. When the player having the knock out causes unnecessary delay, the Referee may throw a ball on the field and call play. No opponent shall come within 50 feet of a player having the knock out, until the ball has been hit.

19.—Whenever a player, either accidentally or intentionally, knocks the ball behind the line, at the end at which the goal defended by his side is situated, it shall be deemed a safety knock out, and shall score one-fourth of one goal against such player's side. When the ball is caromed out or kicked out by a pony it shall not score as above

20.—The Referee shall have power to impose a fine not exceeding forty dollars on any team or member of a team, which shall fail to appear within a reasonable time of the hour named for the events for which they have been entered,

American Polo Association.

or for any misconduct or violation of the rules during the progress of the games, and shall report the same in writing to the Committee for enforcement. And he may exclude from the game any dangerous or vicious pony, and he may start the game notwithstanding the absence of any players after the time fixed.

21.—A player requiring a mallet during the game must ride to the end or side line to procure one; it must not be brought on the field to him.

22.—The Referee may stop the game at any time when the ball is broken, or when it strikes the Referee, or his pony, and may substitute another ball by throwing it between the players at a point as near as possible to where it was stopped.

23.—A ball must go over and clear of the line to be out, and over and clear of the line to count a goal. When a ball is hit above the top of the goal posts, but in the opinion of the Referee through, it shall be considered a goal.

24.—Foul riding is careless and dangerous horsemanship, and lack of consideration for the safety of others. A player in possession of the ball has the right of way, and no one shall cross him unless at such a distance as to avoid all possibility of a collision.

25.—The Referee may suspend a player for the match for a foul, or he may award the opposing side a half goal.

26.—When a player is replaced by a substitute, he cannot return to the team the same day, except to take the place of a player who is incapacitated.

In any change of players after the game has begun, the handicap of the man having the highest number of goals shall be counted.

American Polo Association.

27.—Any member of the Committee may measure ponies (not his own) and issue certificates, good for the season for ponies under five years of age. Ponies five years old or over, holding such certificates, need not be measured again.

28.—No player can play for one prize or more than one team or pair.

29.—No member of a Club which is a member of the Polo Association shall play any match games with or against any Club which is not a member of the Association, nor shall any player play in the team of any Club of which he is not a member, except on written consent of the Committee.

30.—The Polo Association Cups shall not be played for a second time on any ground until all other Association Clubs have had the privilege, providing the grounds of the Club named are equal to the requirements of the Committee.

31.—In drawing teams under the handicap the bye shall be drawn by lot first. In the first round the teams shall be opposed to one another whose total handicap shall be nearest. The day of play for the opposing teams to be decided by lot.

32.—In the event of a game being stopped on account of darkness or for any cause which prevents its being continued the same day, it must be resumed at the point at which it stopped as to score and the position of the ball, at the earliest convenient time, unless settled by mutual agreement between the captains.

33.—A player shall be handicapped with but one Club at a time.

American Polo Association.

34.—The captain of a Club may reserve for any of the Association matches any four players of his Club, including himself, providing such players are notified at least five days before the closing of the entries to the tournament in which such match takes place.

35.—The Polo Association colours are white and dark blue.

PRINCIPAL TOURNAMENTS AND WINNERS.

The following is a list of some of the principal Tournaments and the winners since the date of their inauguration :—

HURLINGHAM OPEN CHAMPION CUP.

Date.	Winners.
1877.	Monmouthshire Club.
1878.	Monmouthshire Club.
1879.	Hurlingham Club.
1880.	Sussex County Club.
1881.	Sussex County Club.
1882.	Sussex County Club.
1883.	Sussex County Club (walked over).
1884.	Freebooters.
1885.	Sussex County Club.
1886.	Freebooters.
1887.	Freebooters.
1888.	Sussex County Club.
1889.	Sussex County Club (walked over).
1890.	Sussex County Club.
1891.	Sussex County Club.
1892.	Sussex County Club.
1893.	Sussex County Club (walked over, but did not take the Cup).
1894.	Freebooters.
1895.	Freebooters.
1896.	Freebooters.

Tournaments and Winners.

Hurlingham Inter-Regimental Tournament.

Date.	Winners.
1878.	5th Lancers.
1879.	5th Lancers.
1880.	16th Lancers.
1881.	16th Lancers.
1882.	5th Lancers.
1883.	7th Hussars.
1884.	7th Hussars.
1885.	7th Hussars.
1886.	7th Hussars.
1887.	5th Lancers.
1888.	10th Hussars.
1889.	9th Lancers.
1890.	9th Lancers.
1891.	9th Lancers.
1892.	13th Hussars.
1893.	10th Hussars.
1894.	13th Hussars.
1895.	13th Hussars.
1896.	9th Lancers.

Hurlingham County Cup.

1885.	Gloucestershire Club.
1886.	Gloucestershire Club.
1887.	Derbyshire County Club (walked over).
1888.	Kent County Club.
1889.	Barton-under-Needwood Club.
1890.	Berkshire County Club.
1891.	Liverpool Club.
1892.	County Meath Club.

Principal Tournaments

Date.	Winners.
1893.	Edinburgh Club.
1894.	Edinburgh Club.
1895.	Rugby Club.
1896.	Stansted.

ALL IRELAND OPEN CUP.

1878.	7th Royal Fusiliers.
1879.	7th Hussars.
1880.	Scots Greys.
1881.	5th Lancers.
1882.	All Ireland Polo Club.
1883.	County Carlow Club.
1884.	5th Lancers.
1885.	Freebooters.
1886.	Freebooters.
1887.	All Ireland Polo Club.
1888.	All Ireland Polo Club.
1889.	Freebooters.
1890.	All Ireland Polo Club.
1891.	13th Hussars.
1892.	9th Lancers.
1893.	13th Hussars.
1894.	15th Hussars.
1895.	Freebooters.
1896.	13th Hussars.

THE ALL IRELAND REGIMENTAL CHALLENGE CUP.

1886.	10th Hussars.
1887.	16th Lancers.
1888.	3rd Hussars.
1889.	4th Hussars.

and Winners.

Date.	Winners.
1890.	4th Hussars.
1891.	15th Hussars.
1892.	13th Hussars.
1893.	9th Lancers.
1894.	10th Hussars.
1895.	13th Hussars.
1896.	10th Hussars.

INDIAN INTER-REGIMENTAL TOURNAMENT.

1877.	9th Lancers.
1878.	9th Lancers.
1879. 1880.	No tournament in these years owing to the Afghan war.
1881.	10th Hussars.
1882.	10th Hussars.
1883.	9th Lancers.
1884.	9th Lancers.
1885.	9th Lancers.
1886.	8th Hussars.
1887.	8th Hussars.
1888.	17th Lancers.
1889.	17th Lancers.
1890.	5th Lancers.
1891.	7th Hussars.
1892.	Queen's Bays.
1893.	Queen's Bays.
1894.	Queen's Bays.
1895.	7th Hussars.
1896.	Durham Light Infantry.
1897.	Durham Light Infantry.

Tournaments and Winners.

Indian Native Cavalry Cup.

Date.	Winners.
1890.	9th Bengal Lancers.
1891.	9th Bengal Lancers.
1892.	14th Bengal Lancers.
1893.	9th Bengal Lancers.
1894.	14th Bengal Lancers.
1895.	18th Bengal Lancers.
1896.	Central India Horse.

Punjaub Tournament.

1886.	12th Bengal Cavalry.
1887.	12th Bengal Cavalry.
1888.	12th Bengal Cavalry.
1889.	12th Bengal Cavalry.
1890.	12th Bengal Cavalry.
1891.	Patiala.
1892.	Patiala.
1893.	Patiala.
1894.	Patiala.
1895.	18th Hussars.
1896.	17th Bengal Cavalry.

Rugby Tournament.

1893.	Rugby Club.
1894.	Cheshire County.
1895.	Freebooters.
1896.	Freebooters.

LIST OF POLO CLUBS.

EUROPE.

ENGLAND.

Aldershot, Divisional.
Barton.
Bowden, Harry E. Gaddum, Esq., Bowden, Cheshire.
Burleigh Park, Blundell Williams, Esq., Stamford.
Cambridge University.
Chester, A. Tyrer, Esq., Plas Newton, Chester.
Chislehurst, Mr. Beck, Sec.
Cirencester, F. J. Townsend, Esq., 1, Ashcroft Villas.
Derbyshire, Earl of Harrington, Elvaston Castle, Derby.
Eastbourne.
Eden Park, Percy Bucknall, Esq., Eden Park, Beckenham.
Fetcham Park.
Hurlingham, Captain Walter Smythe, Polo Manager, Hurlingham Club, Fulham, S.W.
Liverpool, W. Lee Pilkington, Esq., Huyton Grange, near Liverpool.
Ludlow, T. McMicking, Esq., Burway, Ludlow, Salop.
Lyndhurst.
Middlewood.
Monmouthshire, R. W. Kennard, Esq., Llwyn Du, Abergavenny.
North Middlesex, Dr. H. Allen.
Oxford University.
Plymouth.
Ranelagh, E. D. Miller, Esq., Polo Manager, Ranelagh Club, Barn Elms, S.W.

List of

Rugby, W. Bryant, Esq., Spring Hill, Rugby.
Staffordshire, Earl of Shrewsbury and Talbot, Ingestre Hall, Stafford.
Stansted, Tresham Gilbey, Esq., The Grange, Bishop Stortford.
Tiverton, J. de las Casas, Esq., Collipriest, Tiverton.
Warwickshire, P. A. Leaf, Esq., The Brewery, Leamington.
Wellington, A. C. C. Kenyon Fuller, Esq., Finchampstead, Berks
West Essex, Major Tait, Epping.
Wilts, North.
Wirral, F. W. Blain, Esq., Ashfield, Bromborough, Birkenhead.
Woolwich, Captain Head, Royal Artillery Barracks.
Worcestershire, Anthony Lechmere, Esq., Rhydd Court, Worcester.

SCOTLAND.

Edinburgh, J. H. Rutherford, Esq., 14, Great Stuart Street, Edinburgh.

IRELAND.

All Ireland, Major Wood, Diswellstown, Castleknock, co. Dublin.
Antrim, Captain Ivan Richardson, Glenmore, Lisburn, co. Antrim.
Darlow, Stewart Duckett, Esq., Russellstown Park, Carlow.
Fermanagh, T. E. T. Packenham, Esq., Enniskillen.
Freebooters, John Watson, Esq., Bective House, Navan, co. Meath.
Kildare, Colonel de Robeck, Gavan Grange, Naas, co. Kildare.
Londonderry, Andrew Watt, Esq., Londonderry.
Meath, Dr. Sullivan, Meath.

Polo Clubs.

Sligo, R. St. G. Robinson, Esq., Sligo.
Tredeagh (Drogheda).
Westmeath, Captain E. Dease, Earlstown, Goole, Westmeath.

FRANCE.

Deauville.
Paris, M. Kellaire, Pelouse de Bagatelle, Paris.

GIBRALTAR.

Gibraltar, O. W. Thynne, Esq., King's Royal Rifles, Gibraltar.

MALTA.

Malta.

ASIA.

INDIA.

Polo Association of India. Hon. sec., Major Sherston, Rifle Brigade.
Allahabad, Ahmedabad, Bangalore, Bannu, Barrackpur, Bombay Gymkhana, Calcutta, Fort Sandeman, Hyderabad (Deccan), Jhansi.
Jodhpore, Major Beatson, Jodhpore.
Jubbulpore, Kirkee, Kirkee Gymkhana, Karachi, Lucknow, Madras Government House, Madras Gymkhana, Meerut, Mhow, Mian Mir, Ootacamund, Naini Tal, Nusseerabad, Peshawur, Poona Gymkhana, Quetta, Ranikhet, Roorkee, Saugor, Sealkote, Secunderabad, Umballa, Viceroy's Staff.

ASSAM.

Dibrugarh, A. M. Harry, Esq., Dibrugarh.
Jhanzie, F. Perman, Esq., Jhanzie Tea Estate, *viâ* Jorehât.

List of

Jorehât, C. S. Bivar, Esq., Cinnamara, Jorehât.
Lahwal, F. W. Collins, Esq., Bokal, Dibrugarh.
Moran, Secretary, Moran Tea Estate, Sibsagor.
Nazira, J. Hulbert, Esq., Nazira, P.O. Sibsagor.
North Lakhimpur, Secretary, Joyhing.
Nowgong, Secretary, Nowgong.
Nudwa Road, G. W. Sutton, Esq., Dikom, Dibrugarh.
Panitola, A. W. Madden, Esq., Panitola, Dibrugarh.
Rishnauth, Secretary, Rishnauth Estate, Teypur.
Singlo, Secretary, Singlo Tea Estate, Sibsagor.
Teypur, Secretary, Teypur.
Upper Sudiya, F. E. Winsland, Esq., Tippuk, Dibrugarh.

BURMAH.

Rangoon.
Bhamo, Kundat, Mandalay, Maulmain, Meiktila, Moniya, Mugwe, Myingyan, Pokoko, Shewbo, Thayetmo, Toungoo, Yamethin.

AFRICA.

Cairo (Khedivial), E. N. Griffiths, Esq., The Dargle, Natal, Estcourt, Greytown, Government House, Mooi River.
The Rand Polo Club, Charles Jerome, Esq., Johannesburg, Transvaal.

AMERICA.

CANADA AND BRITISH COLUMBIA.

Beaver Creek, M. J. Holland, Esq., Beaver Creek Ranche, Alberta, N.W.T.

Polo Clubs.

Calgary, Alta, T. S. C. See, Esq.
Fort Macleod, E. A. Browning, Esq., Alberta, N.W.T Canada.
High River, Orlando (Florida).
Pincher Creek, E. M. Wilmot, Esq., Pincher Creek, Macleod, Canada.
Qu'Appelle River, Regina, Victoria (B.C.).

United States.

U.S. Polo Association, E. C. Potter, Esq., 36, Wall Street, New York.
Country Club of Brookline, F. Blackwood Fay, Esq., Brookline, Mass.
Country Club of St. Louis, John F. Shepley, Esq., St. Louis, Mass.
Country Club of Westchester, E. C. Potter, Esq., Westchester, New York.
Dedham, Samuel D. Warren, Esq., Dedham, Mass.
Devon (Philadelphia).
Essex County, T. H. P. Farr, Esq., Orange, New Jersey.
Harvard, C. C. Baldwin, Esq., Cambridge, Mass.
Hingham, G. D. Braman, Esq., Hingham, Mass.
Meadow Brook, Oliver W. Bird, Esq., Westbury, Long Island, N.Y.
Monmouth County, P. F. Collier, Esq., Holywood, N.J.
Morris County, Benjamin Nicolls, Esq., Morristown, New Jersey.
Myopia, R. L. Agassiz, Esq., Hamilton, Mass.
Orlando, E. S. Doering, Esq., Orlando, Fla.
Oyster Bay, F. T. Underhill, Esq., Oyster Bay, Long Island, N.Y.
Philadelphia, Charles E. Mather, Esq., Philadelphia, Pa.

List of

Rockaway, John E. Cowdin, Esq., Cedarhurst, Long Island, N.Y.
Tuxedo, Richard Mortimer, Esq., Tuxedo Park, N.Y.
Westchester, A. Rotten, Esq., Westchester.

South America (Argentina).

Association of the River Plate, F. J. Balfour, 559, Piedad.
Belgrano, J. K. Cassels, Lavalle 108, Belgrano.
Bellaco, M. M. C. Henderson, Paysandu.
Camp of Uruguay, L. Edwards, Barrancas Coloradas, Colonia.
Canada de Gomez, J. S. Robinson, C. de Gomez, F.C.C.A.
Casuals, R. McC. Smyth, Venado Tuerto.
Gualeguay, H. J. Perrett, Gualeguay, Entre Rios.
Hurlingham, F. J. Balfour, 559, Piedad, Buenos Ayres.
Jujuy, H. Wright Poore, care of Leach Hnos. y Ca., Salta, Argentina.
La Colina, O. G. Hoare, Santa Rosa, La Colina.
La Merced, P. H. Cawardine, La Merced, Chascomus.
La Victoria, Magnus Fea, Estacion, El Trebol, F.C. Central Argentino.
Las Petacas, Frank E. Kinchant, Las Petacas, San Jorge, F.C.C.A.
Lezama, E. J. Craig, Estancia Las Barrancas, Lezama.
Medie Luna, Scott Moncrieff-Soler, F.C. Pacifico.
Montevideo, Fred. A. Christie, Club Inglés, Montevideo.
North Santa Fé, H. J. J. Bury, Las Limpias, Estacion Carlos Pellegrini, F.C.C.A.
Roldan, W. Ellery, Roldan, F.C.C.A.
Rosario, W. F. Christie, F.C.C.A., Rosario.
San Jorge, G. H. Hall, San Jorge, Estacion Molles, F.C.C. del Uruguay, Montevideo.

Polo Clubs.

Santa Fé, Kemball Cook, Las Tres Lagunas, Las Rosas, F.C.C.A.
Santiago del Estero, Dr. Newman Smith, La Banda, Santiago del Estero.
Tuyu, H. Gibson, Los Ingleses, Ajo, F.C.S.
Venado Tuerto, H. Miles, Venado Tuerto, F.C.S. Santa Fé y Cordoba.

AUSTRALIA.

Adelaide, E. Laughton, Esq., jun.
Argyle, Ballarat, Brisbane, Claude Musson, Esq., 39, Elizabeth Street, Brisbane, Broken Hill, Burra-Caramut Camperdown, Coolak, Cooma, Dubbo, Goulbourn, Hamilton, Ipswich, Melbourne, Muswellbrook, Mount Crawford, Oaklands, Queanbeyan, Quirindi, Scone.
Sydney, Capt. A. J. Dodds, Australian Club, Sydney, N.S. Wales.
Wagga-Wagga, Werribee.

SAMOA.

Apia, T. B. Cusack-Smith, Esq., British Consulate, Apia.

NEW ZEALAND.

Auckland, G. Dennis O'Rorke, The Pah, Onehunga.
Christchurch, R. Heaton Rhodes, Esq., Christchurch, Ashburton.
Hobart Town, Kihi-Kihi, North Canterbury, Poverty Bay Rangiora, Rangitiki, Wanganui, Weikiri.

Dr. NANSEN'S GREAT BOOK.

FARTHEST NORTH.

2 VOLUMES. £2 2s. NET.

Over 100 Full=page and a large number of Text Illustrations.

SIXTEEN COLOURED PLATES in facsimile of Dr. Nansen's own Watercolour, Pastel, and Pencil Sketches.

AN ETCHED PORTRAIT OF THE AUTHOR.

" It is a book for *everybody*—for the explorer, the traveller, and for every *man*, *woman*, and *child* who loves a story of romance and adventure."—*Westminster Gazette.*

"The genius of Defoe could scarcely contrive a more absorbing story than we have in the second volume of the book."—*Spectator.*

" They possess all the fascination of Jules Verne's wonderful stories, with the added interest attaching to them from their being actual performances."—*Literary World.*

THE ALPS FROM END TO END.

BY SIR WILLIAM MARTIN CONWAY.

With 100 Full=page Illustrations by A. D. McCORMICK.

" A high place among these books of climbing which appeal to many who cannot climb, as well as to all who can, will be taken by the very pleasant volume, 'The Alps from End to End.'"—*Times.*

" There is, perhaps, not another living Alpinist—unless we except Mr. Coolidge, who contributes a valuable *précis* of the topography—who could have combined the requisite knowledge with physical capability for the task. . . . Sir William Conway's book is as vivid as it is charming."—*Standard.*

ARCHIBALD CONSTABLE and CO.,
2, Whitehall Gardens, S.W.

THE WHOLE of the
WAVERLEY NOVELS,

Strongly and Tastefully Bound, IN A BOOKCASE COMPLETE, in sets.

CONSTABLE'S REPRINT

OF THE

WAVERLEY NOVELS.

48 Vols., Cloth, Paper Label Title, £3 15s. net, COMPLETE, IN SUITABLE BOOKCASE.

The Author's Favourite Edition

OF

THE WAVERLEY NOVELS.

CONSTABLE'S REPRINT

OF THE

WAVERLEY NOVELS.

The Favourite Edition of Sir Walter Scott.

With all the Original Plates and Vignettes (re-engraved). In 48 Vols. Fcap. 8vo, cloth, paper label title, 1s. 6d. net per volume, or £3 12s. the set. Also cloth gilt, gilt top, 2s. net per volume, or £4 16s. the set; and half-leather gilt, 2s. 6d. net per volume, or £6 the set.

"A delightful reprint. The price is lower than that of many inferior editions."—*Athenæum*.

"The excellence of the print, and the convenient size of the volumes, and the association of this edition with Sir Walter Scott himself, should combine with so moderate a price to secure for this reprint a popularity as great as that which the original edition long and justly enjoyed with former generations and readers."—*Times*.

"This is one of the most charming editions of the Waverley Novels that we know, as well as one of the cheapest in the market."—*Glasgow Herald*.

ARCHIBALD CONSTABLE and CO.,
2, Whitehall Gardens, S.W.

ICE BOUND ON KOLGUEV

A Chapter in the Exploration of Arctic Europe.

To which is added
A Record of the Natural History
of the Island.

BY

AUBYN TREVOR-BATTYE,

B.A., F.L.S., F.Z.S., ETC.,

MEMBER OF THE BRITISH ORNITHOLOGISTS' ASSOCIATION.

With numerous Illustrations by

J. T. NETTLESHIP, CHARLES WHYMPER,
AND THE AUTHOR.

LARGE DEMY 8vo. 21s. NET.

The Spectator.

"From beginning to end the story of this adventure is outside the common lines. 'The idea of the unknown—this it was that attracted me, as it has attracted many people' writes Mr. Battye. This odd corner of the world is a harbourless island with a dangerous coast. It lies well within the Arctic circle, in the part of the Arctic Ocean called Barents' Sea. The old navigators had seen it when trying for the North-East Passage to China, and noted it as a dangerous and desolate island."

The Standard.

"Quite one of the most interesting books of recent travel is Mr. Trevor-Battye's 'Ice-bound on Kolguev.' It is, in truth, a fresh chapter in the exploration of Arctic Europe."

The Times.

" Even in these days of Arctic Exploration the adventures of Mr. Aubyn Trevor-Battye stand out as something unique. His book will take and keep an authoritative position. . . . . A modest and unvarnished picture of pluck and endurance that do honour to the English name."

The Daily Chronicle.

"The book is as attractive to read as this Arctic adventure was risky and original to execute."

The Academy.

"A volume of somewhat unique character, presenting points of interest to the geographer, the naturalist and the ethnologist, while possessing a special charm for the general reader."

The Pall Mall.

" For the manner of Mr. Trevor-Battye's telling we have little but praise. It is graphic, straightforward and never dull. . . . . He gives us a picture which all can realise of life on a barren desert in the Arctic circle, with its wild sleigh rides behind reindeer; its semi-idolatrous worship; its reeking ['choom') interiors, shared by whole families and by fierce wolf-like dogs."

The Saturday Review.

" Extremely interesting notes of the plentiful bird-life and of the necessarily scant flora of this Arctic island add much to the pleasure of an always lively narrative."

The Westminster Gazette.

" Our readers must get the book, and go through it for themselves. To both the naturalist and the man who likes a thrilling narrative it will be alike interesting, and the illustrations and the charming manner in which it has been turned out by the publishers, leave nothing to be desired."

BY THE SAME AUTHOR,

Will shortly be Published,

"AN ARCTIC HIGHWAY OF THE TSAR."

Inscribed by gracious permission

To His Imperial Majesty

THE EMPEROR OF RUSSIA.

ARCHIBALD CONSTABLE and CO.,
2, Whitehall Gardens, S.W.

The Story of an African Crisis

BY

F. E. GARRETT,

The Editor of the *Cape Times*.

The most important book on the recent Jameson Raid, and the Political Attitude of the Transvaal.

Crown 8vo, 3s. 6d.

". . . Mr. Garrett discusses fully, and apparently after access to the best information, the rumours, suggestions and innuendos which have been in the air with regard to the connection of the Colonial Office with the concentration of forces on the Transvaal frontier."—*Daily News.*

"Just the thing that was wanted to enable the ordinary business man to get in a few hours' reading a thorough grip of the events in a history-making episode."—*Financial News.*

"Requires and deserves the most careful perusal."—*South Africa.*

"Fresh matter has been added which gives the work still greater importance."—*Glasgow Evening News.*

"A brilliant piece of political exposition."—*African Critic.*

"The story is here told with local knowledge and as far as possible from first-hand sources of information."—*Financial Times.*

"Any one who wishes to be posted up in matters preceding the Jameson raid and the Johannesburg revolt should read 'The Story of an African Crisis.'"—*Literary World.*

"The re-issue of the work is timely."—*Publishers' Circular.*

"It would take a very clever novelist to have done the work better than Mr. Garrett has himself. . . . Mr. Garrett touches the latest developments of the situation."—*Westminster Budget.*

"We can do no better than recommend every one to read the book. . . . Most novels would come in a poor second."—*Pall Mall Gazette.*

"This terse account of a historic incident."—*Western Press.*

"The account of the Raid and the events preceding and following it is full, readable, and as clear as anything we have seen."—*The Guardian.*

"Eminently topical . . . there ought to be a demand for this."—*Whitehall Review.*

"This attempt at public enlightenment should be at the moment especially useful."—*Liverpool Daily Post.*

"Mr. Garrett has a fine journalistic style, and carries the reader along with him."—*Highland News.*

"It is a wonderful book, and ought to be read by every one who has the slightest interest in Africa."—*Land and Water.*

"Mr. Garrett has been to an exceptional degree behind the scenes."—*The Bookseller.*

"Shows the author's thorough knowledge and perfect command of his subject."—*The Colonies and India.*

". . . Probably the most valuable contribution yet made to the literature of the Transvaal Question."—*Black and White.*

"The whole story is told from beginning to end . . . many interesting details appear for the first time."—*The Stock Exchange.*

"The best book on the subject."—*Morning Post.*

"The book presents a deal of fresh matter, and the whole is very interesting to follow."—*Belfast News Letter.*

ARCHIBALD CONSTABLE & CO.,
WESTMINSTER.

CONSTABLE'S
Hand Atlas of India

A NEW SERIES of Sixty Maps and Plans prepared from Ordnance and other Surveys under the direction of

J. G. BARTHOLOMEW, F.R.G.S., F.R.S.E., Etc.

In half-morocco, or full-bound cloth, gilt top, 14s.

The Topographical Section Maps are an accurate reduction of the Survey of India, and contain all the places described in Sir W. W. Hunter's "Gazetteer of India," according to his spelling.

The Military, Railway, Telegraph, and Mission Station Maps are designed to meet the requirements of the Military and Civil Service, also missionaries and business men who at present have no means of obtaining the information they require in a handy form.

The index contains upwards of ten thousand names, and will be found more complete than any yet attempted on a similar scale.

Further to increase the utility of the work as a reference volume, an abstract of the 1891 Census has been added.

"Nothing half so useful has been done for many years to help both the traveller in India and the student at home. ' Constable's Hand Atlas' is a pleasure to hold and to turn over."—*Athenæum.*

ARCHIBALD CONSTABLE & CO.,
WESTMINSTER.

"The Game of Polo"

BY

T. F. DALE

(*"Stoneclink" of "The Field"*),

Containing a large number of full-page sepia plates, illustrative of celebrated ponies, many text illustrations

BY

CUTHBERT BRADLEY, L. C. SMYTHE, and others,

and a photogravure portrait

OF

MR. JOHN WATSON.

Demy 8vo. One Guinea net.

"Stoneclink" of *The Field*, as an authority on the Game of Polo, needs no introduction to devotees of this national pastime.

The author in this volume treats very fully of the game in all its aspects. Starting with its early history, he traces the spread of its popularity down to the present time, when hardly any centre of importance in England, India, Australia, South Africa and America is without its Polo Club.

Great consideration is given to the breeding of ponies, their stable management, training, and the general care required in their education.

Mr. Dale also goes fully into the training and qualifications necessary for the players.

ARCHIBALD CONSTABLE & CO.,
WESTMINSTER.

FRIDTJOF NANSEN'S

"Farthest North"

Being the narrative of the Voyage and Exploration of the *Fram*, 1893-96;

AND

The Fifteen Months' Sledge Expedition by

DR. NANSEN AND LIEUT. JOHANSEN;

With an appendix by OTTO SVERDRUP.

About One Hundred and Twenty Full-Page and Numerous Text Illustrations.

SIXTEEN COLOURED PLATES

IN FACSIMILE FROM

DR. NANSEN'S OWN SKETCHES.

Portrait, Photogravures, and Maps.

2 *vols. large demy 8vo, Two Guineas net.*

"Altogether it is not too much to say that the book is a masterpiece of story-telling."—*Times*.

"Certainly it will remain for many a year to come as an Arctic classic, and the narrative which beats its record will be the sensation of a future age."—*Academy*.

"The genius of a Defoe could scarcely contrive a more absorbing story than we have in the second volume of the book."—*Spectator*.

"Dr. Nansen is a writer of singular capacity; he enlists the sympathies of his readers and makes their hearts go out to him."—*Athenæum*.

ARCHIBALD CONSTABLE & CO.,
WESTMINSTER.

Ice-bound on Kolguev

A Chapter in the Exploration of
Arctic Europe.

TO WHICH IS ADDED A RECORD OF THE NATURAL HISTORY
OF THE ISLAND.

BY

AUBYN TREVOR-BATTYE,
B.A., F.L.S., F.Z.S., ETC.,
MEMBER OF THE BRITISH ORNITHOLOGISTS' UNION.

With numerous Illustrations by
J. T. NETTLESHIP, CHARLES WHYMPER,
and the Author.

"From beginning to end, the story of this adventure is outside the common lines."—*The Spectator.*

"Quite one of the most interesting books of recent travel is Mr. Trevor-Battye's 'Ice-bound on Kolguev.'"—*The Standard.*

"His book will take and keep an authoritative position. . . . A modest and unvarnished picture of pluck and endurance that do honour to the English name."—*The Times.*

"The book is as attractive to read as this Arctic adventure was risky and original to execute."—*The Daily Chronicle.*

"Possessing a special charm for the general reader."—*The Academy.*

"An admirable record of Samoyed life, manners and customs, with chapters on the botany, zoology, geology, language, etc., of the island."—*The Daily News.*

"It is graphic, straightforward, and never dull. . . ."—*The Pall Mall.*

"Extremely interesting. . . . A well-got-up, well-printed and well-illustrated book."—*The Saturday Review.*

"Our readers must get the book and go through it for themselves. . . . Leaves nothing to be desired."—*The Westminster Gazette.*

"The courage with which, in the interests of science, Mr. Trevor-Battye and his companion took their chance of worse fortune deserves, as it has received, the admiration of all capable of appreciating what might have been their fate had the Samoyedi not been met with."—*The Athenæum.*

ARCHIBALD CONSTABLE & CO,
WESTMINSTER.

THIRD EDITION, NOW READY.
REVISED AND BROUGHT UP TO DATE.

Popular Readings in Science

BY

JOHN GALL, M.A., LL.B.,
Late Professor of Mathematics and Physics,
Canning College, Lucknow,

AND

DAVID ROBERTSON, M.A., LL.B., B.Sc.

With many Diagrams, a Glossary of Technical Terms, and an Index.

Crown 8vo, pp. 468. *Price* 4s.

"The authors lay no claim to originality, but have exercised a judicious choice in the selection of subject matter. . . . The narrative style which has been adopted by the authors will make the book acceptable to general readers who are anxious to make acquaintance with modern science."—*Nature.*

"We have been gratified by the unvarying excellence of the work, which we cordially recommend as likely to advance the cause of science."—*Practical Teacher.*

"Full of interesting and instructive information. . . . The perusal of it will give considerable enjoyment and instruction to all who take it up."—*Educational News.*

"A popular manual of science, not only extremely correct in its facts, but abundantly instructive and interesting. A book such as this has long been needed."—*Liberal.*

ARCHIBALD CONSTABLE & CO.,
WESTMINSTER.

CONSTABLE'S LIBRARY OF

Historical Novels and Romances

EDITED BY LAURENCE GOMME

Crown 8vo, 3s. 6d., cloth.

The First of the Series

Harold : The Last of the Saxons

BY LORD LYTTON

Crown 8vo, cloth extra. After a Design by A. A. TURBAYNE.

The value which this series must possess for educational purposes has influenced to a very considerable extent the plan adopted by the editor for presenting each volume to the public. The well-known attraction of a good historical novel to the young will be made use of to direct attention to the real history of the period of which each story was intended by its author to be a representation. To refer the reader to the genuine authorities of the period ; to give as far as possible a short account of the period, and of the characters introduced ; to present illustrations of costume, buildings, and facsimiles of signatures ; and to give examples of the language of the period, is not only to introduce young students to these books as interesting examples of English literature and phases of English literary history, but to bring home to them, in connection with pleasant associations, most of the really important events in English history. Every reign, practically, will be represented by at least one story, and sometimes by more than one, and in this way the series will gradually take the reader through the entire annals of English history.

For the purpose of school libraries, as school prizes, for holiday tasks, and as gifts to children, the series will place at the disposal of teachers, parents, guardians, and friends a class of books which is not only entirely distinct from any that has hitherto done duty in these respects, but is also very much needed.

It has been decided to commence the series with the most important epoch of English history, namely the Norman Conquest ; but this will not preclude the issue at convenient times of books which relate to earlier British history or to foreign history.

HAROLD will be followed by—

WILLIAM I. : Macfarlane's *Camp of Refuge*, 1844.

WILLIAM II. : *Rufus or the Red King*, 1838 (Anonymous).

STEPHEN : Macfarlane's *Legend of Reading Abbey*, 1845.

ARCHIBALD CONSTABLE & CO.,
WESTMINSTER.

Boswell's Life of Johnson

Edited by AUGUSTINE BIRRELL.
With Frontispieces by ALEX ANSTED, a reproduction of Sir JOSHUA REYNOLDS' Portrait.

Six Volumes. Foolscap 8vo. Cloth, paper label, or gilt extra, 2s. net per Volume. Also half morocco, 3s. net per Volume. Sold in Sets only.

"Far and away the best Boswell, I should say, for the ordinary book-lover now on the market."—*Illustrated London News.*

". . . We have good reason to be thankful for an edition of a very useful and attractive kind."—*Spectator.*

"The volumes, which are light, and so well bound that they open easily anywhere, are exceedingly pleasant to handle and read."—*St. James's Budget.*

"This undertaking of the publishers ought to be certain of success."—*The Bookseller.*

"Read him at once if you have hitherto refrained from that exhilarating and most varied entertainment; or, have you read him?—then read him again."—*The Speaker.*

"Constable's edition will long remain the best both for the general reader and the scholar."—*Review of Reviews.*

In 48 *Volumes*

CONSTABLE'S REPRINT
OF
The Waverley Novels

THE FAVOURITE EDITION OF
SIR WALTER SCOTT.

With all the original Plates and Vignettes (Re-engraved). In 48 Vols.

Foolscap 8vo. Cloth, paper label title, 1s. 6d. net per Volume, or £3 12s. the Set. Also cloth gilt, gilt top, 2s. net per Volume, or £4 16s. the Set; and half leather gilt, 2s. 6d. net per Volume, or £6 the Set.

"A delightful reprint. The price is lower than that of many inferior editions."—*Athenæum.*

"The excellence of the print, and the convenient size of the volumes, and the association of this edition with Sir Walter Scott himself, should combine with so moderate a price to secure for this reprint a popularity as great as that which the original editions long and fully enjoyed with former generations of readers."—*The Times.*

"This is one of the most charming editions of the Waverley Novels that we know, as well as one of the cheapest in the market."—*Glasgow Herald.*

"Very attractive reprints."—*The Speaker.*

". . . Messrs. Constable & Co. have done good service to the reading world in reprinting them."—*Daily Chronicle.*

"The set presents a magnificent appearance on the bookshelf."—*Black and White.*

ARCHIBALD CONSTABLE & CO.,
WESTMINSTER.

The only Complete Uniform Edition of the Works of George Meredith

32 *Volumes.* *Demy 8vo.* 10s. 6d. *a Volume.* *Sold in Sets Only.*

This Edition is limited to 1,000 numbered and signed Sets for sale. The First Volume contains a PORTRAIT, reproduced in Photogravure, from a drawing specially made for this Edition by JOHN S. SARGENT, A.R.A.

Extracts from a Leading Article which appeared in the *Daily Chronicle*, November 20th, 1896:—

Two companion volumes have been issued this week which may serve as what MATTHEW ARNOLD was fond of calling a *point de rèpere*, a guiding mark in English literature. "The Works of George Meredith," Vols. 1 and 2 (Westminster: ARCHIBALD CONSTABLE & Co.), mean more, vastly more, than a handsome addition to the library shelves. They are a formal recognition that Mr. MEREDITH has at last come into his own, tangible evidence of reputation long in the making now triumphantly crowned. A note to the volumes, whose contents are, "The Ordeal of Richard Feverel," tells us that the novel was originally published in 1859. . . . When POPE, enquiring for the author of "London," was told that the poem was by an obscure young man, one JOHNSON, he remarked that the young man "would soon be *déterré*." But there was no POPE in Mr. MEREDITH'S case, and many a long year elapsed before he was "unearthed." To-day, by the general consent of the English-speaking world, or of that part of it at any rate which concerns itself with the humaner letters, he is accepted as our foremost living novelist, with THOMAS HARDY by his side. There are few things in literary history more curious than the emergence of Mr. MEREDITH from prolonged obscurity, first into the position of a much discussed but little read author—fanatically worshipped by a small clique, as fanatically reviled by the outside world—and finally into assured and universal fame. Something of the kind there was perhaps in SHAKESPEARE'S case, and something too in GOLDSMITH'S. . . . If there be any one who still doubts the practical influence of literary criticism upon the "general reader," he has striking proof of it here. The victory of Mr. MEREDITH is also a victory for the critics. It was a few hardy pioneers, with Mr. SWINBURNE at their head, and Mr. STEVENSON, Mr. HENLEY, and Mr. BARRIE of their company, who "discovered" Mr. MEREDITH, and insisted in season and out of season that the world at large should share the fruits of their discovery.

. . . He can give you the most poignant, heart-rending tragedy in a "Rhoda Fleming," the most generous, Molièresque comedy in "Evan Harrington." Is there a more exquisite love-idyll in the language than that of "Richard Feverel"? A more terrible exposure of human weakness—all SWIFT'S irony without his savagery—than "The Egotist"? In "Shagpat" has he not beaten the Arabian Nights on their own ground? Is there a more brilliant exploit in the grotesque-pathetic than "Harry Richmond"? His books are studies of the will-to-live in all its various incarnations—young women and old men, "roaring human boys" and cranky sea-dogs, pedants, men-about-town, "fine old English gentlemen," tailors rustics, demagogues, adventurers, and even wet-nurses. And he paints them all, not in the dull photographer's monochrome that the mere realist affects, but in rich warm colours from a full palette.

Extract from a Special Article in *The Westminster Gazette*, December 1st, 1896:—

Once more we are impressed with the essential sincerity of Mr. Meredith's writing. However much it is written from the head—and the intellectual pleasure of it is immense—it is also written from the heart.

The size is convenient, the cover simple and good, the paper of the best, and the printing so brilliant that you might suppose it to come straight from a hand press.

"Mr. Meredith's most fervent worshipper could not desire a more charming edition of his works to read and reverence."—*The Scotsman.*

"Mr. Meredith, who in generous youth gave to the world an imperishable literature, in full maturity of judgment confirms the now inalienable gift."—*The Academy.*

ARCHIBALD CONSTABLE & CO.,
WESTMINSTER.

Imperial Defence

By the Right Honourable SIR CHARLES WENTWORTH DILKE, Bart., M.P., and SPENSER WILKINSON.
New Edition, Revised and in part re-written.
12mo, *cloth*, 2s. 6d.

THE CRISIS IN THE EAST. England's Position. Read

The Nation's Awakening

By SPENSER WILKINSON.
Crown 8vo, cloth, 3s. 6d.

"A large part of the present book has already appeared in the columns of one of your contemporaries, but some of the most interesting chapters . . . appear for the first time in this volume. He deals reasonably and sensibly with our relations with the United States. Mr. Wilkinson . . . leads up to the proposed system of alliances, in which, taken as a whole, . . . I accept all the steps by which he arrives at it."—SIR CHARLES DILKE in *The Daily Chronicle,* July 1, 1896.

"It will be seen that Mr. Wilkinson's programme is not lacking in ambition. . . . his pages contain many pregnant suggestions, and much food for reflection."
—*The Times.*

The Brain of an Army

A Popular Account of the German General Staff.
By SPENSER WILKINSON.
New Edition, with Letters from COUNT MOLTKE and LORD ROBERTS.
With Three Plans. Crown 8vo, 2s. 6d.

The Volunteers and the National Defence.

By SPENSER WILKINSON,
Formerly Captain 20th Lancashire R.V. Author of "The Brain of an Army."
Crown 8vo, 2s. 6d.

Problems of the Far East

Japan—Korea—China.
New and Cheaper Edition, Revised and brought up to date, with a New Chapter on the late War in the East.
By the RT. HON. GEORGE N. CURZON, M.P.
Fellow of All Souls' College, Oxford; Author of "Russia in Central Asia" and "Persia."
With Numerous Illustrations and Maps. Extra Crown 8vo, 7s. 6d.

"A valuable addition to the literature dealing with the problems of the Far East."
Morning Post.

The Key of the Pacific:

The Nicaragua Canal.
By ARCHIBALD R. COLQUHOUN, F.R.G.S.
Gold Medallist of the Royal Geographical Society; Special Correspondent of the *Times.*

Large Demy 8vo, with Maps and Illustrations, 21s. net.

"A repertory at once copious and authoritative of such information as is needed to enable the reader to form an adequate opinion of the feasibility and advantages or otherwise of the Nicaragua Canal."—*Times.*

ARCHIBALD CONSTABLE & CO.,
WESTMINSTER.

CONSTABLE'S SIX SHILLING NOVELS

In the Tideway
By FLORA ANNIE STEEL.

The Folly of Pen Harrington
By JULIAN STURGIS.

Sister Jane
By "UNCLE REMUS"

"Shows the hand of a master."—*The New Saturday.*
"Of all Mr. Harris's recent stories 'Sister Jane' is the best."—*Academy.*
"Mr. Harris's delightful story."—*Literary World.*
"A charming book. A most engaging book."—*Daily Chronicle.*

Green Fire : A Story of the Western Islands
By FIONA MACLEOD, Author of "The Sin Eater," "Pharais," "The Mountain Lovers," etc.

"There are few in whose hands the pure threads have been so skilfully and delicately woven as they have in Fiona Macleod's."—*Pall Mall Gazette.*
"The fuller revelation which we looked for from Miss Fiona Macleod's earlier works has been amply fulfilled in this volume."—*Western Mail.*

The Amazing Marriage
By GEORGE MEREDITH. *Fourth Edition.*

"To say that Mr. Meredith is at his best in 'The Amazing Marriage' is to say that he has given us a masterpiece."—*Daily News.*

The Tragic Comedians
By GEORGE MEREDITH. Crown 8vo.

The Enemies : A Novel
By E. H. COOPER, Author of "Richard Escott," etc.

"A well-written and interesting book."—*Manchester Courier.*

The Vigil : A Romance of Zulu Life
By CHARLES MONTAGUE.
With Full-page Illustrations by A. D. M'CORMICK.

"His story is a strong and humanly interesting one, told in a direct and forcible manner. . . . An excellent story."—*Athenæum.*

His Vindication : A Novel
By MRS. NEWMAN,
Author of "Too Late," "Jean," and "The Last of the Haddons."
"The virtues of Mrs. Newman's work are decidedly not common."—*Daily Chronicle.*

ARCHIBALD CONSTABLE & CO.,
WESTMINSTER.

CONSTABLE'S THREE AND SIXPENNY
SERIES

His Majesty's Greatest Subject
A NOVEL. By S. S. THORBURN, I.C.S.

Chin-Chin-Wa
By CHARLES HANNAN, F.R.G.S.

"Chin-Chin-Wa is a cleverly realised study of an Englishman who turns Chinaman."—*Daily Chronicle.*
"Delightful and dramatic."—*British Review.*

A Sturdy Beggar and Lady Bramber's Ghost
TWO STORIES BY CHARLES CHARRINGTON.

"Two stories full of merit."—*Western Mail.*
"An original turn of thought, and a vivacious style."—*The Globe.*

Tales of South Africa
By H. A. BRYDEN,
Author of "*Gun and Camera in South Africa,*" "*Kloof and Karroo,*" *etc.*

"These admirably told tales give a better conception of the life of the wanderer in South Africa than any formal book of travels. We can hardly speak too cordially of the little volume."—*Spectator.*

The Shoulder of Shasta
By BRAM STOKER.

"Mr. Bram Stoker's story is unflagging, full of vigour, and capital reading from end to end ; moreover, it conveys a vivid picture of life and manners in a corner of the world better known to him than to the majority of those who will read his book."—*Standard.*

Dramas of To-Day
By NELLA PARKER.

"They combine brevity with artistic completeness and concentration of interest. . . . The power displayed of vividly presenting dramatic situations and characters is excellent."—*Scotsman.*

James; or, Virtue Rewarded
By the Author of "Muggleton College."

"An exceedingly smart satire upon modern Church life of the over-organized kind. We cannot pretend to like it. . . . We wish we could say that the sermon of the warden lacked justification."—*Guardian.*
"A most amusing novel. Clever, caustic, and amusing."—*Nottingham Guardian.*
"'James is really wonderful. . . . A book to be read.'"—*Birmingham Post.*
"A decided hit. . . . An exceptionally clever story."—*Glasgow Herald.*

ARCHIBALD CONSTABLE & CO.,
WESTMINSTER.

CONSTABLE'S HALF-CROWN SERIES

A Writer of Fiction   A Novel.
By CLIVE HOLLAND,
Author of "My Japanese Wife." Cloth extra.

"It is a striking story, told with restraint and considerable power."—*Pall Mall Gazette.*

The Love of an Obsolete Woman
CHRONICLED BY HERSELF.
Cloth extra.

Madge o' the Pool
By WILLIAM SHARP.
Fcap. 8vo.

" It would be hard to point to anything more brilliant or more satisfactory amongst the writers of Mr. Sharp's generation."—*Glasgow Herald.*
" Of unusual merit."—*Daily Mail.*
" Fresh and notable work."—*The Globe.*
" Really excellent work."—*Manchester Guardian.*

Hans van Donder
A Romance of Boer Life.
By CHARLES MONTAGUE,
Author of " The Vigil."

"Mr. Montague has written another charming romance."—*Scotsman.*
"Admirably told. The descriptions of Big Game Shooting are highly exciting."—*Glasgow Herald.*

Torriba
By JOHN CAMERON GRANT.

" Torriba is unquestionably bold in treatment and well written."—*Globe.*

ARCHIBALD CONSTABLE & CO.,
WESTMINSTER.

THE ACME LIBRARY

Paper, 1s.; cloth extra, gilt, 2s.

"The Acme Library makes a promising start."—*The Publishers' Circular.*
"The Acme promises to be a notable series."—*Cheltenham Chronicle.*

The Parasite
By A. CONAN DOYLE.
Third Edition.

"Nothing so startling has appeared since Mr. Stevenson's 'Dr. Jekyll and Mr. Hyde.'"—*Literary World.*
"Cleverly written, and will be found effective."—*Globe.*
"For a railway journey, or an hour or two of leisure, there could hardly be a more delightful volume."—*Bookseller.*
"An ideal book for a long railway journey."—*Weekly Sun.*
"A series of vivid impressions and strange events."—*Dundee Advertiser.*
"The story is thrilling."—*Manchester Courier.*
"A truly thrilling tale."—*Glasgow Herald.*

The Watter's Mou'
By BRAM STOKER.
Second Edition.

"It is excellent."—*Punch.*
"A thrilling story of the very best type."—*Yorkshire Post.*
"The setting of the tale is perfect. . . . The few types of people are real and living. . . . The proportions and the interdependence of this tragedy are classic."—*World.*
"A little drama in itself."—*Globe.*
"An excellent and pathetic sketch."—*Glasgow Herald.*
"We commend it to the public on account of its high literary merit."—*Irish Times.*
"A spirited and touching story of faithful and enduring love."—*Saturday Review.*
"A neat and touching piece of work."—*Weekly Sun.*

A Question of Colour
By F. C. PHILIPS,
Author of "As in a Looking-Glass."

"As clever and as closely interesting a short story as could be desired. . . . A well-executed piece of fiction."—*Dundee Advertiser.*
"Powerful and impressive."—*Bristol Mercury.*
"Mr. Philips is seen at his very best in the latest addition to this series. Brilliantly written, and full of strong situations."—*Glasgow Herald.*
"Strong, skilful, and thrillingly told."—*Morning Leader.*

From Shadow to Sunlight
By THE MARQUIS OF LORNE, K.T.

"Will be read with interest by every one who takes it up."—*Scotsman.*
"An entertaining little book."—*Daily Telegraph.*
"A slight but prettily executed drama."—*St. James's Gazette.*

ARCHIBALD CONSTABLE & CO.,
WESTMINSTER.

The Acme Library, *continued*

A Bubble
By L. B. WALFORD,
Author of "Mr. Smith."

"Pleasantly characteristic of its author."—*Globe.*
"A delightful little social study, written in the author's happiest vein. Takes rank amongst her best efforts, and should find general appreciation."—*Nottingham Guardian.*
"A charming little book, written quite in Mrs. Walford's best manner."—*National Observer.*

An Impressionist Diary
By HELMUTH SCHWARTZE.

"The charm of the 'Diary' lies in the style, in the pretty descriptive passages, and in the sketches of amusing incidents and people."—*Scotsman.*
"The secondary characters in the book are out of the common and very well drawn, while the artist colony of Austell Bay is touched off in true impressionist style."—*Liverpool Post.*

The Red Spell
By FRANCIS GRIBBLE.

"A very successful work."—*Nottingham Guardian.*
"A vivid and picturesque sketch."—*Glasgow Herald.*
"A very dramatic little tale."—*Daily Graphic.*
"The sketch is fascinating, and is drawn with rough vigour and great power."—*Manchester Courier.*
"A subject of grim fascination, and he has handled it with supreme skill. . . . An absorbing story."—*The Weekly Sun.*

Dr. Koomadhi of Ashantee
By FRANKFORT MOORE.

An Engagement
By SIR ROBERT PEEL, Bart.

A Feminine Conviction
By GEORGE ST. GEORGE.

Angela's Lovers
By DOROTHEA GERARD.

ARCHIBALD CONSTABLE & CO.,
WESTMINSTER.

Some Books of Travel and Adventure

New Edition. Profusely Illustrated, 7s. 6d. net.

The Western Avernus
Toil and Travel in Further North America.
By MORLEY ROBERTS.

Crown 8vo, cloth gilt, with Illustrations by A. D. MCCORMICK, *and from photographs. 7s. 6d. net.*

"Interesting to all. . . . Capitally illustrated."—*St. James's Budget.*
"Will hold the reader thrallbound."—*Publisher's Circular.*

The Alps from End to End
Second Edition. Large Demy 8vo. Price One Guinea net.
By SIR WILLIAM MARTIN CONWAY.
With 100 full-page Illustrations by A. D. MCCORMICK.

"A high place among these books of climbing which appeal to many who cannot climb, as well as to all who can, will be taken by the very pleasant volume, 'The Alps from End to End.'"—*Times.*

"There is, perhaps, not another living Alpinist—unless we except Mr. Coolidge, who contributes a valuable *précis* of the topography—who could have combined the requisite knowledge with physical capacity for the task. . . . Sir William Conway's book is as valid as it is charming."—*Standard.*

Second Edition. Large Demy 8vo, cloth, gilt top, One Guinea net.

Ice-Bound on Kolguev
By AUBYN TREVOR-BATTYE, F.L.S., F.Z.S., Etc.
With numerous Illustrations by J. T. NETTLESHIP, CHARLES WHYMPER, and Drawings by the Author and ED. THORNTON, and three Maps.

"His book will take and keep an authoritative position. . . ."
"Ought to be secure of a welcome from a very large number of readers."—*The Times.*

". . . The book is as attractive to read as this Arctic adventure was risky and original to execute."—*Daily Chronicle.*

Travels in the East
OF
NICHOLAS II., EMPEROR OF RUSSIA
(When Cesarewitch, 1890–91).

Written by Order of His Imperial Majesty by PRINCE E. OOKHTOMSKY, and translated from the Russian by ROBERT GOODLET, St. Petersburg, and Edited by Sir GEORGE BIRDWOOD, M.D., K.C.I.E. *With about 500 Illustrations engraved on wood, and numerous heliogravure plates. 2 vols., £5 5s. net.*

"Published in the most sumptuous form, the first volume of a translation of Prince E. Ookhtomsky's authorised narrative of His Majesty's travels in the East, in 1890–91, when he was Cesarewitch."—*Times.*

". . . A word of high praise is due to Messrs. Constable for the external graces of this publication, which is one of the finest specimens of luxurious printing we have ever seen."—*Daily Chronicle.*

"We like the Czar's book. . . . It abounds in living interest from its first page to its last. Finally, we have to congratulate Messrs. Constable on the splendid printing and illustration of this work"—*Daily News.*

ARCHIBALD CONSTABLE & CO.,
WESTMINSTER.

FORTHCOMING BOOKS

Selected Poems
By GEORGE MEREDITH

Dracula
By BRAM STOKER

The Household of the Lafayettes
By EDITH SICHEL

War Medals
By JOHN HORSLEY MAYO

Highland Tales and Legends
By the MARQUIS OF LORNE

In the Tideway
By FLORA ANNIE STEEL, Author of "On the Face of the Waters"

Jack Smith M P
By HYDE MYDDLETON

ARCHIBALD CONSTABLE & CO.,
WESTMINSTER.

SOME BOOKS FOR THE LIBRARY

A Book for Dante Students.

The Chronicle of Villani
Translated by ROSE E. SELFE.
Ed ted by the REV. P. H. WICKSTEED. *Crown 8vo, 6s.*

"The book, picturesque and instructive reading as it is, is not less interesting and still more valuable, for readers of Italy's greatest poet."—*Scotsman.*

"Sure to have a warm welcome."—*Globe.*

"A thoughtful introduction gives a general outline of the Florentine problems of the period."—*Western Morning News.*

Spenser's Faerie Queene
Edited by KATE M. WARREN.
Fscap. 8vo. Vol. i. [*Just ready.*

English Schools. 1546-1548
By A. F. LEACH, M.A., F.S.A.
Late Fellow of All Souls', Oxford, Assist. Charity Commissioner. *Demy 8vo.*

This work shows, by records hitherto unpublished and for the most part unknown, that there was a widespread and effective provision in England for Secondary Education before the Reformation, which was destroyed or marred in efficiency under Henry VIII. and Edward VI., especially by the Act for the Confiscation of Colleges and Charities. Edward VI., indeed, instead of being, as commonly reputed, the founder, ought rather to be regarded as the destroyer of schools. Some light is also thrown on how far he is to be regarded as restorer of what was destroyed.

The Preaching of Islam
By T. W. ARNOLD, B.A. *With Two Maps. Demy 8vo, 12s.*

This is a work on the spread of the Muhammadan religion by missionary methods. It is a subject that has not as yet met with adequate treatment, and the author of this book, having been for many years a professor in a Muhammadan college in India, has had special opportunities for pursuing his investigations. Mr. Arnold's work is no way controversial, but aims at giving as complete an account as possible of the actual facts of the missionary history of Islam. This faith is commonly said to have been spread by the sword; but those who make this statement (and indeed those few who have denied it) have not hitherto attempted to collect together the historical evidence necessary for forming any legitimate judgment on the subject. This the author has tried to do after a lengthy study of the literature of the subject in many languages, including much unpublished MS. material. The work attempts to cover the whole of Muhammadan history, so far as the missionary activity of Islam is concerned, in all the countries into which this religion has penetrated.

"One of the most elaborate and careful accounts of the spread of Mahomedanism that we remember to have seen in any language. As Professor Arnold rightly says, his subject is a vast one. The writer has condensed into less than 400 pages a mass of material that might have alarmed a German Professor, let alone an English one."—*The Times.*

The Popular Religion and Folklore of Northern India By WILLIAM CROOKE.
With Numerous Full-page Plates. Two Vols. Demy 8vo.

Highland Dress, Arms, and Ornament
By the RIGHT HON. LORD ARCHIBALD CAMPBELL.
With Numerous Illustrations. Demy 8vo.

ARCHIBALD CONSTABLE & CO.,
WESTMINSTER.

The Popular Religion and Folklore of Northern India

By WILLIAM CROOKE.

With numerous Full-page Plates. Two Vols. Demy 8vo. 21s. net.

"The author of these important volumes has honourable place among those who have utilised opportunities for study of the complex social and religious life of the Hindu."—*Daily Chronicle.*

"Mr. Crooke's labours of collection and disposition with incidental critical suggestion and comparative illustration deserve the most liberal recognition."—*New Saturday.*

"The book is in every respect an admirable one, full of insight and knowledge at first hand."—*Times.*

The Preaching of Islam

By T. W. ARNOLD, B.A.

With Two Maps. Demy 8vo. 12s. net.

"One of the most elaborate and careful accounts of the spread of Mahomedanism that we remember to have seen in any language. As Professor Arnold rightly says, his subject is a vast one. The writer has condensed into less than 400 pages a mass of material that might have alarmed a German Professor, let alone an English one."—*The Times.*

"A scholarly and extremely interesting volume. . . . A highly valuable contribution to knowledge of the history of Mohammedanism."—*Glasgow Herald.*

"This is a history of the missionary aspect of the religion. . . . As a proof and picture of the extraordinary missionary enterprise of the Muhammedans, the book makes interesting reading."—*Scotsman.*

"There has been no English book on Mahomedanism printed since the well-known Dictionary that is so informing and suggestive as this of Mr. Arnold's. This book is wanted. It is highly instructive, being clear, well arranged, and readable."—*Manchester Guardian.*

"An intelligent, accurate and well-written history of the propagation of the Muslim faith. . . . Well digested and carefully put together,—in a word, an important contribution to the literature bearing on the Muslim faith."—*Publishers' Circular.*

ARCHIBALD CONSTABLE & CO.,
WESTMINSTER.

Tales of South Africa

BY

H. A. BRYDEN,

Author of "Gun and Camera in South Africa,"
"Kloof and Karroo," etc.

Crown 8vo, 3s. 6d.

"All are excellent. . . . 'A Bushwoman's Romance' is a powerful and pathetic story of love amongst the low-grade natives of Central Southern Africa. . . . Haggard has done nothing better, and few things as good."—*African Critic.*

"We can hardly speak too cordially of the volume."—*Spectator.*

"There is a fine wild gamey flavour about Mr. Bryden's stories. He is a hunter, and a close observer of nature."—*Scotsman.*

"Mr. Bryden is establishing a claim to be considered the Hardy of South Africa."—*African Review.*

"His stories are enthralling."—*Academy.*

"Excellent stories. . . . All come as veritable breaths from the Veldt."—*Cape Times.*

"As pictures of Boer and Veldt life they are convincing."—*Land and Water.*

ARCHIBALD CONSTABLE & CO.,
WESTMINSTER.

At all Booksellers and Bookstalls.

NEW AND CHEAPER EDITION,

REVISED AND BROUGHT UP TO DATE,

WITH A NEW CHAPTER ON THE LATE WAR IN THE EAST.

Problems of the Far East

Japan—Corea—China

BY THE

Rt. Hon. GEORGE N. CURZON, M.P.

With numerous Illustrations and Maps. Extra Crown 8vo, 7s. 6d.

"Certainly the influence of Mr. Curzon's thoughtful generalizations, based as they are upon wide knowledge, and expressed in clear and picturesque language, cannot fail to assist in solving the problems of the Far East."—*Manchester Courier.*

"We dealt so fully with the other contents of Mr. Curzon's volume at the time of first publication, that it is only necessary to say that the extreme interest and importance of them is enhanced by recent events, and the light of which they are revised."—*Glasgow Herald.*

"Any one who desires to know anything of Japan, Corea, and China, will employ time profitably in becoming acquainted with Mr. Curzon's book. The book is thoughtfully and carefully written, and the writer's well-known abilities, both as a traveller and a statesman, lend weight to his words, while the fact that it is already in its fourth edition shows that the public realize its value."—*Belfast News Letter.*

"All who have read the volume will admit that it is a valuable addition to the literature dealing with the problems of the Far East."—*Morning Post.*

"His impressions of travel, confirmed by a study of the best authorities, are interesting and well written."—*Manchester Guardian.*

"'Problems of the Far East' is most informing, and deserves to be widely read."—*Liverpool Mercury.*

ARCHIBALD CONSTABLE & CO.,
WESTMINSTER.

THE

Command of the Sea

By SPENSER WILKINSON

Crown 8vo, Coloured Wrapper, 1s.

CONTENTS.

SEA POWER AND LAND POWER.	THE SECRET OF SUCCESS.
NATIONAL POLICY.	READINESS IN THE RIGHT PLACE.
THE MEDITERRANEAN.	THE ACTUAL SITUATION.
DEFENCE BY A NAVY.	A SPECIFIC PROPOSAL.

"What is Unionism to an Empire shaken, or Home Rule to four impoverished nations, or an eight hours' day to working classes thrown out of employment, or Socialism to a people fighting for its life? . . . There are still some thousands of Englishmen to whom the security of the Empire is dearer than the most highly advertised party nostrums."

"Mr. Wilkinson expounds with great force and felicity of illustration the true meaning of the strategical expression 'The Command of the Sea.'"—*The Times.*

"Mr. Wilkinson treats the subject with a clearness and grasp almost above praise; within 100 brief pages he condenses all that the average citizen requires to enable him to form a reasonable judgment on the needs of our navy to maintain that command of the sea on which, as he clearly shows, our very existence now depends. More than this, he comes forward with a distinct and practical suggestion, which, if adopted by the nation, will ensure the provision of a fleet and army competent to fulfil the duties for which they exist."—*The Journal of the Royal United Service Institution.*

"Very able essays."—*The United Service Gazette.*

"Good sense at last."—*The Realm.*

ARCHIBALD CONSTABLE & CO.,
WESTMINSTER.

THE
Brain of an Army

A POPULAR ACCOUNT OF THE GERMAN GENERAL STAFF.

By SPENSER WILKINSON.

New Edition, with Letters from COUNT MOLTKE *and* LORD ROBERTS.

With Three Plans. Crown 8vo, 2s. 6d.

"A model of clearness in exposition. There is not a dull page in the book."—*Pall Mall Gazette.*

"The best manual that exists of the functions of a general staff."—*Athenæum.*

"We should like to call the attention of our readers to the important preface which Mr. Spenser Wilkinson has added to the new edition of his fascinating and most valuable little book, 'The Brain of an Army.' Mr. Wilkinson's competence to speak on these matters has been vouched for by Moltke himself, and needs no words from us."—*From an article on the "Reorganization of the War Office" in the "Spectator."*

"Not only a popular, but a thorough account of the nature of the German General Staff. . . . Its author has entered into the spirit of the German Army in a manner we should hardly have believed to be possible for a foreigner."—*Deutsche Rundschau.*

"He has not only mastered all its material by careful study, but has acquired such a living knowledge of his subject as a foreigner rarely attains."—*Kölnische Zeitung.*

"A book full of thought. . . . The author shows that he is very intimate with our military institutions as regards the training of the army to be a manageable instrument of war, and the education of officers for the higher commands."—*Jahrbücher für die Deutsche Armee und Marine.*

"That he most perfectly commands his subject is shown by the opening pages, and the light which he throws upon the German General Staff (which he calls 'The Brain of an Army') loses none of its strength until he has successfully accomplished in brief and convincing style the task which he has undertaken."—*Internationale Revue über die Gesammten Armeen und Flotten.*

"Deserves to be better known among us than it is, for it presents the essence of that organ, the German General Staff, with rare clearness and accuracy, and with an understanding and a technical knowledge which in a foreigner, and one who according to our notions is not a professional soldier, are in a high degree surprising."—*From an article on Spenser Wilkinson's works in the "Militar Wochenblatt."*

ARCHIBALD CONSTABLE & CO.,
WESTMINSTER.

The Waterloo Campaign, 1815

By CAPTAIN WILLIAM SIBORNE.

Fourth Edition. Crown 8vo. 832 pages. 13 Medallion Portraits of Generals. 15 Maps and Plans. Bound in Red Cloth, gilt top, 5s. net.

"The best general account of its subject that has been written, whether for a soldier or for a general reader; and its appearance in the handy and well-printed volume in which it is now issued will be welcome to many."—*Scotsman.*

"It is charmingly written, is graphic, yet precise, and abundantly witnesses to the author's most strenuous endeavour to do justice to every one who took part in that great conflict."—*Birmingham Post.*

"Many books have been written upon this fertile theme, but it is doubtful if a more faithful and comprehensive account has ever been given to the world, and for this reason we welcome its re-appearance in a fourth edition."—*Liverpool Daily Post.*

"Another notable reprint. . . . There can be no doubt that the narrative is a classic in its way."—*Globe.*

"The most comprehensive account in the English language of the Waterloo Campaign. The editing, as one would expect, is conscientious and accurate, and the volume is well illustrated with portraits and plans."—*Glasgow Herald.*

AN AUTHENTIC NARRATIVE OF
The Death of Lord Nelson,
21st October, 1805.

By WILLIAM BEATTY, M.D., Surgeon of H.M.S. *Victory*.

Second Edition. Crown 8vo. Two Illustrations. 2s. 6d. net.

"It is an old story, but the account of the Death of Nelson, by Dr. Beatty, the Surgeon of the *Victory*, which has just been reissued in Arber's Reprints, is an exceedingly interesting one."—*Westminster Gazette.*

"Professor Arber has added an interesting little volume to his series of reprints. It is the 'Authentic Narrative of the Death of Lord Nelson, with the circumstances preceding, attending, and subsequent to, that event; the professional report of his Lordship's wound, and several interesting Anecdotes.' . . . The little volume contains several illustrations, two of which are very striking. They represent the ball which mortally wounded Nelson, in the exact state in which it was extracted, and the same ball set in crystal, as it is now preserved in the Armoury at Windsor Castle."—*Glasgow Herald.*

ARCHIBALD CONSTABLE & CO.,
WESTMINSTER.

Milton Keynes UK
Ingram Content Group UK Ltd.
UKHW051527160424
441253UK00002B/52